TESTIMONIALS

"From the day I first met Heather, I knew she was a champion of and for women … a protector of the vulnerable and a resource for healing, a guide and natural mentor. Her commitment to making women stronger through financial confidence and freedom comes from a place of selfless passion. Heather has successfully integrated the conversations and feelings women have regarding money with a holistic view on self-care and well-being. This book takes a scary topic for many women and provides easy-to-follow tools, exercises, and rituals to achieve financial wellness and confidence."

—**Molly Anderson**
Vice President, Sales and Programming, Canyon Ranch

"In her new book, Heather Ettinger has made a compelling case for real change in the financial services industry. *Lumination* highlights how the traditional, transactional world of finance has failed to meet the needs of 51 percent of the American population, and then offers a framework for women who want to have more meaningful conversations about wealth and financial well-being with each other, their families, and their advisors."

—**Kathleen Burns Kingsbury**
Wealth psychology expert and author of
*Breaking Money Silence®: How to Shatter Money Taboos,
Talk More Openly about Finances, and Live a Richer Life*

"The entire financial services industry has missed the mark on diversity and inclusion and how they serve the needs of women and minorities. Today, leadership matters more than ever before. With her new book, *Luminations*, Heather Ettinger is leading a movement to help women step forward.

"As with any movement, it will gain no traction unless the leaders are authentic. Heather always brings her authentic self, with a growth mindset, and lives the words and behaviors that support doing what is right for her family, customers, partners, and community at large. As the CEO and Chief Cheerleader at *Racing Toward Diversity* magazine, I am one of her biggest fans!"

—**Fields Jackson, Jr.**
Founder & CEO, *Racing Toward Diversity*

"Women have known forever that one size does not fit all. In her enlightened perspective on financial wellness, Ettinger uses her years of expertise in the male-dominated world of financial management to find a voice that resonates with women. Instead of regarding financial literacy as an isolated skill set, Ettinger helps us navigate and integrate our financial life into our sense of self, utilizing our individual circumstances, time of life, values, and dreams to make informed choices. Clear, concise, and empathic, this volume educates, illuminates, and provides actionable steps to achieve financial independence and fluency."

—**Bettina Katz, PhD**

"Every now and then a book comes along that is a real life-changer. One that sets in motion an awakening of awareness, insight, and understanding of certain critical aspects of our lives that we have never explored before, or if we have, not in great depth. Heather has written and gifted us with just such a book. *Lumination* is not only a life-changer, but in some cases a life-saver. She shines light into all the dark, scary corners of our financial obstacles and conditioning, and attitudes that prevent us from becoming and being our very best financially well selves. ... She also helps us learn to become 'wholly well' in many other aspects of our lives. This is an absolute must-have guide that every woman should read—in any circumstance and at any age—written with incredible knowledge, expertise, and love. Thank you, Heather."

—**Roxanne Kaufman Elliott**
President & CEO, ProLaureate Ltd

"Heather is helping women all over the United States unlock our silence, and ask for what we want, to get what we need, to achieve financial wellness. It is an inspiring work that provides practical and impactful tools to help women achieve their financial and attitudinal wealth, with the gift of self-assurance by the end of the journey."

—**Susan E. Kay**
Vice President, MFS Investment Management

"From the first sentence, Heather Ettinger draws you into this book, hinting that the information you are about to read is not only important but will somehow improve your life. She does not disappoint. *Lumination* both acknowledges and respects what women experience and lights a path forward toward true financial wellness. Reading this book will not only make you feel understood, but also relieved, empowered, and connected."

—**Julie Littlechild**
Founder & CEO, Absolute Engagement

"Integrity, Perseverance, and Honesty are three of the core values prominent in the Life Skills curriculum in my daily work as the Executive Director of First Tee, Cleveland. They are also the values that are at the core of Heather's moral compass. I have known Heather for over 30 years, and she has always been laser-focused on creating strategies to help and support women and girls both in financial literacy and opportunities to build confidence on their life's journey.

"Heather found this focus and passion locally over the past three decades and it has organically grown to regional, national, and international scale. Heather's success has been driven by the success of those whom she has inspired. It's contagious.

"First Tee has a unique partnership with LPGA*USGA Girls Golf to empower girls through the game of golf and inspire them to dream *big*. Heather uses the same type of empowerment through shining the light on financial literacy for women and girls.

"*Lumination* can be the nudge and resource that so many women need in order to truly embrace both knowledge and insight in their own financial acumen."

—**Patricia LoPresti**
Executive Director, First Tee, Cleveland

"*Lumination* is a practical guide for women who want to take control of their money but don't know where to begin. Part workbook, part autobiography—this book will help retrain your brain on the power and possibilities of a dollar bill."

—**Kristen Lucas**
Chief Marketing Officer, Luma Wealth Advisors

"Heather Ettinger is the real deal and, in this book, she is a pure truth-teller. The prescription she writes for women surrounding our financial health is transparent and authentic. I saw my past, my present, and my opportunity to craft a smart financial future."

—**Margaret Mitchell**
President & CEO, YWCA Greater Cleveland

"*Lumination* should be required reading for everyone—not just women. Heather's ability to reveal the power that women harness, the headspace we occupy, and our desire to be our best selves leaps off every page. She understands our 'origin story'—how we got here, but more importantly, how we are moving toward becoming the most influential force in all spending and investing decisions. Her firm understanding of our collective experience inspires boldness and strength. Heather says it best: 'With the support of men and women who want a healthier approach to financial well-being, together, we can forge a new path.' A path that, in my opinion, has been a long time in coming."

—Stephanie Silverman
Cofounder, Your Teen Media

"*Lumination* is illuminating! Written with both passion and expertise, wealth management thought-leader Heather Ettinger highlights the importance of why the discussion around women and money should focus on financial wellness rather than just financial resources. Through both real-life examples and a practical step-by-step guide, *Lumination* provides women of all ages a perfect read that addresses important topics: from understanding your money history and values, to instituting an attainable plan for success. There is no better time than now for women and girls to become financially empowered and this book helps them do just that."

—Suzanne Siracuse
CEO, Suzanne Siracuse Consulting Services, LLC

"In her newest book, *Lumination*, Heather Ettinger is directing her message to women and the financial professionals who hope to serve them. The book highlights the economic power of women throughout their lifecycle, but also acknowledges that as a group, many women lack the fundamentals of financial literacy that would help them to take firm control of their financial lives. Ettinger cleverly links the Four Pillars of Financial Fitness and personal wellness (balance, stamina, flexibility, and strength) with anecdotes drawn from women she has worked with and her own experiences.

"This is certainly a book by a woman for women. But the insights it provides are also critical lessons for parents, teachers, advisors, and the entire financial services industry."

—Mark Tibergien
Retired CEO,
Pershing Advisor Solutions, a BNY Mellon Company

"Heather's passion and wisdom surrounding women and their wealth journey is apparent in every page of this book. I was able to see my past and present in many of the pages, which helped me feel 'normal', but the most exciting pages were the pages that gave me a glimpse into my future.... My bigger, brighter 'illuminated' future. Reading this book is like having a conversation with Heather. And since that's one of my favorite things, I now see myself as very lucky ... to be able to pick up the book, and chat with my most valuable advisor."

—Jill Young
Certified EOS Implementer, Author, and Speaker

LUMINATION

LUMINATION

SHINING A LIGHT ON
A **WOMAN'S JOURNEY** TO
FINANCIAL WELLNESS

HEATHER ETTINGER

ACADEMY
PRESS

For permission requests, write to the below address:

Lumination Enterprises
c/o Heather Ettinger
22550 Shelburne Road
Shaker Heights, OH 44122
heather@heatherettinger.com

The opinions expressed by the Author are not necessarily those held by PYP Academy Press.

Ordering Information: Quantity sales and special discounts are available on quantity purchases by corporations, associations, and others. For details, contact Heather Ettinger at the above address.

Edited by: Gina Sartirana and Nancy Crompton
Cover design by: Nelly Murariu
Typeset by: Medlar Publishing Solutions Pvt Ltd., India

Printed in the United States of America.
ISBN: 978-1-951591-44-1 (hardcover)
ISBN: 978-1-951591-43-4 (paperback)
ISBN: 978-1-951591-45-8 (ebook)

Library of Congress Control Number: 2020916210

First edition, October 2020.

The information contained within this book is strictly for informational purposes. The material may include information, products, or services by third parties. As such, the Author and Publisher do not assume responsibility or liability for any third-party material or opinions. The publisher is not responsible for websites (or their content) that are not owned by the publisher. Readers are advised to do their own due diligence when it comes to making decisions.

The mission of Publish Your Purpose Press is to discover and publish authors who are striving to make a difference in the world. We give marginalized voices power and a stage to share their stories, speak their truth, and impact their communities. Do you have a book idea you would like us to consider publishing? Please visit PublishYourPurposePress.com for more information.

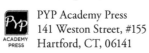
PYP Academy Press
141 Weston Street, #155
Hartford, CT, 06141

DEDICATION

This book is dedicated to all the women who have lived in fear or apprehension that they haven't done enough to manage their finances, who feel trapped because they don't have financial freedom, and those who may have started the work but aren't sure they are on the right path or working with the right people. As young girls, we receive money messages that forever impact our relationship with money. Often, we are told that we aren't good with math or won't be good at managing our funds. Nothing could be farther from the truth. In my over 30-year career in advising clients, I can tell you women are great at managing finances and creating a holistic plan. When women are given a chance to explore in a safe environment what is important and how best to make choices for them and their family, they thrive.

May this book shine a light for you on the possibilities.

TABLE OF CONTENTS

PART III:
THE BUILDING BLOCKS

PART IV:
ASSESSING YOUR INFLUENCERS AND
INFLUENCES ON THE SIX AREAS OF YOUR LIFE

PART V:
BUILDING YOUR LUMINATION PLAN

"Everyone shines, given the right lighting."

—Susan Cain

INTRODUCTION

You have a unique story—past, present, and future. Two of the three chapters are written. But the future is a blank canvas where you can make changes to create your path to financial wellness.

In the United States, over 70% of people, regardless of socio-economic status, say their greatest source of stress is financial. We don't have a path to achieving financial wellness because a lack of time and/or good guidance has prohibited us from reaching that summit. Here is the good news: this book offers you an opportunity to explore that "future" chapter in an inviting, clear, and practical way.

Often, I start my financial literacy programs with a cartoon that reads "Men, if you want to understand a woman's brain, imagine a browser with 2,468 tabs open-All at the same time! All the time!" This book understands that women have different challenges and priorities than men when it comes to achieving financial wellness. We have a more comprehensive list of concerns and worries that must be addressed before any of those browser tabs can be closed.

Mother, Wife, Daughter, Sister, Aunt, Friend, Pioneer, Mentor, Leader, Visionary, Caregiver, Dreamer, Entrepreneur, Philanthropist, Advisor, Coach, Problem Solver, Financial Wellness Architect, Connector, Strategist, Writer, Sports Enthusiast, Teammate, Ice Hockey Player, Connector, Skier, Hiker, Cyclist, Adventure Seeker, World Traveler, Wine Enthusiast, and Champion for Women and Girls—this is who I am on any given day! How about you? We all play many roles daily, especially women. Life is full of planned and unplanned life transitions. Some create challenges and barriers; some create opportunities.

Why am I writing this book? The answer is simple yet complicated at the same time. The complexity comes from two sources. One is that our society discourages talk about financial details and views financial discussion as distasteful. Caitlin Zaloom, an anthropologist at New York University, describes how money taboos emanate from the widely held belief that "your value as a human being is somehow made material in your pay and in your accounts."[1] In fact, our society is more comfortable talking with friends about marital discord, mental health, addiction, race, sex, and politics than money. The second reason is that the financial advisory business has failed to build trust with the public: because their compensation and delivery have been more focused on how much money you have than on what you want for your life. In general, there is

---

[1] Quoted in "Why So Many Americans Don't Talk About Money" by Joe Pinsker. The Atlantic.com/family/archive/20202/03/americans-don't-talk-about-money-taboo/607273/ (accessed August 6, 2020).

a focus on investments and "winners and losers." Most advisors fail to address how your resources can be guided to help you live life in your best intentional way. In addition, many advisors also come across as condescending and salesy. For these reasons, there is a gap between what individuals want and need and what is being delivered by advisors. This gap leads to individuals distrusting that advisors hear them, understand them, or have their best interests in mind.

| | |

Why is this a book written for women by women? Both the research and my experience over the past 35 years of working with female clients indicate that the time has come for a change. Women want hyper-personalized outcomes-based financial advice that meets their real-life goals. They don't necessarily want a female advisor, but they do want someone to whom they can relate, who understands their unique situation and "clicks" with them and their family. The emphasis must be about the individual woman's real life, not only on the money. And women now have the power, which I will illustrate, to get what they need and want.

It is time to change the way we think about and talk about our relationship to money, and that is the simple reason for me writing this book. I want to shine a light on how we can have a healthier relationship with our money by exploring more about our "why," or our values, designing our "what," which is our intentional life, and realizing that the "how" is financial and human capital. Importantly, your money is not what defines you, your happiness, or your impact on the world. Rather, it is your "why" and the "what" or the actions that you take every day to support and demonstrate your core values. This is how you shine your light out on to the world.

Alicia Keys wrote recently, "If you love someone, you love their journey."[2] We all have different life journeys. My career—including coauthoring two industry-changing studies with Eileen O'Connor, "Women of Wealth: Why Does the Financial Services Industry Still Not Hear Them?" and "Women of Wealth: What Do Breadwinner Women Want?"[3]—has been focused on the need for financial industry advisors to understand that women are all different and need to own our journey. To help guide you and create space to explore your world, I will share my own journey and a few stories from my friends along their journeys. I am doing what I hope that you will do: be vulnerable, be open to exploration, and be willing to pivot to live a more intentional and fulfilling life for you.

| | |

No one will ever take your money more seriously than you. It is time for you to claim ownership of your money and finances. You deserve clarity, transparent dialogue, and a plan with priorities and goals clearly aligned with your resources in order to achieve a happy and healthy life plan.

Throughout this book, you will have a series of stories to read, questions to answer, and exercises to open your mind and develop your lens to build a process to live your intentional and "well" life. You will delve into your own "money journey and money code." You will explore your wealth through a view of both human capital and financial capital. You will learn how to unlock the toxic pieces of your life and find more of the joy in the affirmative, energy-creating

---

[2] Alicia Keys with Michelle Burford, *More Myself: A Journey*. New York: Flatiron Books, 2020.

[3] https://lumawealth.com/category/research.html

areas, and positive people and influences in your life. Most important, you will learn how to address and create solutions that help you avoid your bad behaviors and habits when triggers pop up.

The Lumination process will change your dialogue around and relationship with money—the thoughts, emotions, and conditioning that drives your behavior. You may choose to do every exercise or pick those that resonate most with you. My hope is that this will be a book that you come back to whenever you feel a need to reflect and get some clarity, or perhaps to pivot and refocus on the best version of you and your life.

Lumination is about shining a light on that best version of you. By shining a light, we chase out the shadows. Do not be afraid of the brightness; you have so much to offer this world.

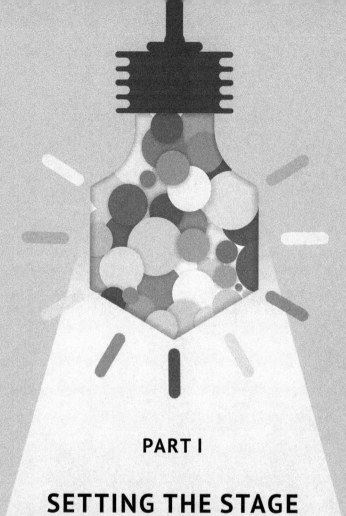

PART I

SETTING THE STAGE

*"If you don't like the road you're walking,
start paving another one."*

—Dolly Parton

CHAPTER ONE

BEGINNING THE JOURNEY: THE AUTHOR'S STORY

As a child, I was never one to take the traditional path. Growing up with older brothers, I was daring and a risk-taker. My father raised me as he did the boys. As such, I was not the "typical girl" and instead preferred to explore new ground, push boundaries, or do the unexpected! For example, I grew up getting signed up for sports like ballet and figure skating. However, without a graceful bone in my body, I quickly realized that I would never excel at any of those sports. Because much of my time at home was spent playing outdoor sports in the back yard with my brothers, including baseball, soccer, football, and street hockey, I pushed to join boys teams or at least play on the "pioneering" girls teams. Pursuing these sports made me much happier even though it was not a common path for girls of my age.

It was important for me to pursue this nontraditional path because I went from feeling "less" than, due to my lack of grace, to feeling a sense of accomplishment in sports that involved more aggressiveness. It was OK to be different. While this reflection included sports for me, most of us find ourselves exploring new skills and passions. This is especially true when what we are doing is not "clicking" for us. We can discover new things that bring us a sense of fulfillment and achievement. The message is that we often have to try new things in order to grow, and perhaps travel down a different path than what is expected.

Similarly, in my academics and my summer jobs, I tried a variety of positions and pushed for new opportunities to learn. For example, over most of my youth, my father had our family host the young adult children of his overseas clients at our home during the summer while they worked as interns for his investment company. Always curious, I asked my father if I could go overseas and work for one or two of those large financial institutions and stay with *their* family. While we had always been on the receiving end of these relationships, I was intrigued to learn more about the world outside the United States. At first, my father was taken aback that I was so bold as a young woman to think about traveling alone. However, he came around to appreciating that I wanted to seize such a phenomenal opportunity. Perhaps he was also happy because I had his pioneering genes!

That summer opened my eyes to differences in culture, history, and bias around the world. I worked in both London and Geneva as an intern. When I worked in London, it was the summer of the Hyde Park and Green Park bombings by the Irish Republic Army and, to compound things, the unions running the public transportation (The Tube) and trains were on strike. Terrorism was part of the culture and daily life, something I had not experienced in the United States. Further, working as an investment intern, I learned how these activities impacted the financial markets, even in that pre-internet age. Even then, there were dramatic actions taken in response to current events and threats. Out of my home cocoon, I realized that I had much to learn about people, world cultures, and behaviors. I also had a lot to learn about myself. Most important, I learned that on any day, an event or choice taken by people out of your control could dramatically change your life.

As I write this book, we are living through the quarantine of COVID-19. This event has forever changed all our lives. We deal with many unknowns and uncertainty in what were our routines and daily life. Much of this generates a feeling of loss and anxiety, and rightfully so. However, like any new situation that we are presented with, it is a time of learning about life and, most notably, about ourselves. It is a very good time to reflect on our responses and choices as we move forward. What will now have more meaning and be more appreciated? How can we change for the better? We will be shining a light on our new paths, and we can always learn at any age. Our past and this experience will be forever entwined with our future choices.

When I graduated from college, I boldly stated that one day I wanted to be an equity trader in Boston. Why Boston? Well, I wanted to go into the same industry that my father was in and wanted to develop my own reputation, independent of him. He was a self-made success, had a strong personality, and, certainly for me and others, often a presence that was larger than life. He did not have connections in Boston as he did in other cities like New York City. I also wanted a major financial city because I wanted a cutting-edge environment. In addition, I was an ice hockey player, and in 1983 Boston was one of the few cities where I could continue to play on a competitive level with other women. Again, I was choosing a pioneering path, independent of the easy path where my father could be influential. Strong-willed and determined, I became an equity trader in Boston, a major financial city that I did not know at all, where my father had no connections and where I could play ice hockey!

In 1987, after a successful start to my career by many measures, I moved back to Cleveland, Ohio. I would pivot from a focus on just my career and success to wanting to make a more significant impact, both professionally and personally. Without understanding what my bigger purpose may be, I began exploring several different organizations and associations where I found passion. Perhaps because I was the product of a girl's school education, or because I was a pioneer in my own choices, I explored several different organizations that were advancing the interests of women and girls. I soon met three passionate philanthropists—Ellie Gerson, Marge Carlson, and Janie Kirkham—who would forever change my life and career. These women shared with me that only 6% of national funding was going to programs that addressed the needs of women and girls. More important, they taught me that if we educated and empowered women about their money, women could be the agents of social change. I was intrigued, to say the least.

With my background and desire to help drive change, I committed to creating financial literacy programs to connect women and open them to learning how to manage their financial lives best. It was a magical partnership. My mentors shared their own journeys openly with families that did not discuss money and how they were changing their own behaviors and values to have those important conversations. Looking back, I realize that they were role models for me and the generations of women who would come after them. Combining their life experience and wisdom around the power of intentional giving, with my fundamentals of building financial literacy, resilience, and strength, we had a recipe for success and meaning for women. I am forever thankful for these women who opened my eyes to a path for change. Sadly, none of them are still with us, but their legacy lives on in me and others. That is the definition of a true legacy of impact.

| | |

Throughout my life, I have admired my mother, who is a smart, cultured woman. She is a student of all art forms, most especially theatre and literature, attentive to detail, beautiful, funny, fun-loving, and the most thoughtful person I know. She remembers everyone's birthday, writes the most beautiful cards and notes, and is the queen of both small and large gestures of kindness. It was not until this last decade that I have come to appreciate how adventuresome she has been. You see, my mom was typical of her generation and told to have her place, that she should not or could not manage finances and that she should always present a certain image. As such, she and I had a formal relationship for many years. She did not learn how to be vulnerable with me until more recently. Finally, I have taken the time to ask more questions about her life and listen deeply to her stories and memories. I am learning about who she is and what she really feels and cares about the most. I am grateful that we have had this chapter in our lives, where we have learned and enjoyed so much more of each other.

When my mom became a widow of a man who was larger than life and the love of her life, she was initially lost. However, she has surprised me and others in many ways over the past couple of years. She has developed her intentional life, more limited with age, yet more focused on what she can control and what brings her joy. She has also learned that she can manage finances! She has overcome her history of negative money messages and opened herself to explore her true skills and capabilities. Despite more life challenges, including some forgetfulness, she continues to find time to reach out to those who helped her to express gratitude for their assistance.

Yes, she is the most thoughtful person that I know. I always thought that I was a Daddy's girl, but I now realize that I am most certainly a mix of both of my parents. As I reflected on my "why" for writing this book, it is a combination of both my parent's influence. My father encouraged and supported my work with women and their families because he also noticed the condescending and belittling behavior shown toward women. In addition, I more recently watched my mother's money journey, going from feeling inadequate due to her inherited money to learning that her life is hers to control. Her journey is an excellent example of refocusing on values and what she needs to give her joy at this point in her life. I want more women to have this life-changing perspective earlier in their lives.

The best decision of my life was choosing my husband, Jeff. There are no words to describe this man's unwavering support for my dreams. The first time my mom met him, she described him as "a secure guy," one who did not need to prove his masculinity or power. He was secure in who he was and what he brought to our relationship. Like every couple, we have had our moments and challenges! But we talk, we get help when we need it, and we put our relationship and support for each other at the center of our world. Because, at the end of the day, we are each other's centering force and recharging station.

Jeff will not be happy that I have highlighted him in this book, but I must because he is a critical part of my journey. He has had to live the ups and downs and discrimination against me, promises made and promises broken, and my relentless push to move forward. I have leaned hard on him. Most of the world sees me as strong and fiercely independent. The way that I get there, however, is by having a partner who challenges, but also hugs me and holds me tight when life is hard. He fills me with courage and love, and I hope and work hard to do the same for him every day. He has taught me that this is how we build a partnership of mutual love and respect.

Together we have raised two independently minded daughters and an enlightened son. I say that because our biggest challenge and greatest reward has been the journey of raising three kids who have good values and are good people. Our daughters and son will continue our commitment to empowering women long after we are gone because they know it is the right thing to do. Everyone should feel valued and loved. After all, part of the "Lumination" journey is shining a light on those relationships that we cherish most.

*"The most common way people give up their power
is by thinking they don't have any."*

—Alice Walker

CHAPTER TWO

THE "AGE OF WOMEN" OPENS THE DOOR FOR CHANGE

Over the last three-plus decades as a financial advisor, wife, parent, daughter, caregiver, executive, innovator, philanthropist, and entrepreneur, I learned that all paths have speed bumps and roadblocks. Life interferes with our best intentions. I never expected the deep-rooted discrimination and bias against women in the workplace and our communities, how raising three kids would be my worst and best work, and that juggling the role of a caregiver for parents would be the hardest challenge of my life. But all these paths opened my learning to better choices and better solutions, and the opportunity to share and help others with my lessons learned.

Today, I am a better advisor because I have experienced challenges and transitions in my own life as well as helping and coaching clients through their life journeys and transitions, planned and unplanned. In this book, I will share lessons learned, challenges and opportunities, and how all of this has led me to believe we can change how we dialogue as a society in a way that better resonates and supports women, men, girls, and boys. We all together, can have a more inclusive approach.

| | |

We have a financial wellness crisis in this country. It begins with women being underserved but extends much deeper. Neglecting financial wellness, due to the gap in delivery of an understandable and clear approach by financial advisors, affects us all.

The following statistics shed more light on this subject:

- 71% of workers say financial stress is their most common cause of stress.[4]
- On average workers lose 13 hours of productivity per month due to financial concerns.[5]
- The most common reason given for divorce after infidelity is financial stress.[6]

The time has come to change the way we see and manage our money discussions. Most families avoid any discussion about money

---

[4] Consumer Financial Protection Bureau. https://www.consumerfinance.gov/ (accessed August 6, 2020).

[5] Mercer: Inside Employees Minds, *Financial Wellness*, Vol 2, 2017.

[6] Rachel Cruze, *Ramsey Solutions: The State of Finances in the American Household*, 2017.

and planning. That leaves the discussion to being driven by the financial services industry. Most providers of financial advice use jargon, sell products, focus on "beating the market" versus meeting financial goals, and ignore or speak to women in a condescending way. All these factors leave individuals, and especially women dissatisfied. A PIMCO study in 2018 reported that over half of the approximately 750 women surveyed said that the financial services industry does not reflect their lifestyles or services. In addition, 78% of these women said that they would be more interested in talking to an advisor if they focused on improving their quality of life, versus just beating the market.

Women are often the leaders of family discussions around finances. Women control over half the wealth in this country. Moreover, 90% of women will control the family finances at some point in their lives. They also make the bulk of the purchasing decisions for the family. Thus, it is critical that the financial services industry, ranked as one of the worst in meeting women's needs, change their behavior to be more holistic and inclusive.

- Women are more likely to want to work with an advisor, but only 20% do![7]
- Over a third of women said that they had been patronized when dealing with the financial services industry.[8]

---

[7] Jessica Bennett and Jesse Ellison, "Women Will Rule the World." *Newsweek* (July 5, 2010). https://www.newsweek.com/women-will-rule-world-74603 (accessed August 6, 2020).

[8] WealthiHer Network Report, 2019: Understanding the Diversity of Women's Wealth. https://www.kleinworthambros.com/fileadmin/user_upload/kleinworthambros/pdf/The_WealthiHer_Network_Report_2019.pdf (accessed August 6, 2020).

- Half of the women surveyed in a multiyear study by New York Life Investments said their financial advisor is incapable of connecting with them on a personal level by taking the time to understand their specific needs.

| | |

In the current approach of most advisors, the process of discovery with new clients is very uncomfortable and exposes more about our fears and vulnerabilities than our hopes and dreams. Advisors begin by asking how much money you have, which immediately puts clients on the defensive, feeling like there isn't enough or they haven't done enough to save and/or be prudent with resources. Clients immediately feel judged or inadequate even if they have a lot of money because they don't know what is expected or why the discussion starts with how much they have versus what they want or need. More often, this approach leads to quickly assessing our inadequacies and us feeling discouraged. Instead, we need to begin by building a base of understanding and trust.

In order to feel valued, safe, and understood, the process should begin with an advisor asking thoughtful questions and thoroughly listening to the potential client to learn more about them, their family, and their life journey. Learning family history, current situation, and future plans or dreams is critical. Learning about the limitations and challenges they have faced or expect to face is critical. Exploring dynamics around money conversations in the family is important. Who has been involved and who should be involved in the future may require some coaching and additional tactics and resources. The focus of advisors should be on how individuals and families can reach their goals in a thoughtful and supportive way.

| | |

Talking about money for any of us feels like we are getting financially "naked" and exposes our true vulnerabilities. If we feel judged or that we aren't meeting some arbitrary expectation of having enough to warrant an advisor's time, we won't be open and honest enough to explore for ourselves or with advisor's assistance our challenges and opportunities. The better process and framework for advisors with prospective clients is to change the process and the framework of these discussions to focus more time and energy on substantial and thoughtful dialogue. It will require great listening and more emotional intelligence along with the technical skills for an advisor to create a stronger relationship. It may take longer, but it will be a more meaningful and rewarding journey of exploration and discovery for all, and especially for the client.

We must change the dialogue to focus on financial wellness rather than just financial resources. Financial wellness is at the intersection of wealth and wellness in our lives. Wealth or how much money you have is not the "what," it is the "how" and involves both financial capital and human capital. But you cannot direct your "how" without knowing your "why" and your "what." This book will give you a process to explore these areas in your own life, creating your own customized financial wellness plan. Remember, this is a journey, not a destination.

Financial wellness is the intersection of wealth and your physical and mental health. It is where you have both tangible and attitudinal wealth. It is built through financial education and literacy, aligning your resources to your personal values and priorities, and understanding your choices and trade-offs. In this way it aligns your mind, body, and true wealth. Financial wellness is a state or process that brings you three benefits: Education, Empowerment, and the ability to Embrace your life choices.

Because of the growing influence of women—who, in fact make the majority of consumer and healthcare purchasing decisions for the family, attain a higher proportion of college and graduate degrees, and build wealth at a disproportionately faster rate than men—many are calling this the Age of Women, or The Female Economy. Women will continue to grow their influence on family purchasing decisions for products and services. Their opinions, preferences, and influence will dramatically affect every industry, especially financial services. We will see more alignment of decisions and purchases around positive impact and social change.

Women are often the center or core of the family life, whether in a partnership, married, divorced, widowed, or single. They have more power than they realize and are the agents of social change. Women control over half of the wealth in the United States, are starting companies at a rate of 4-to-1 over men, and are the lead breadwinners in over 40% of households. Further, in terms of impact, if you give a dollar to a woman, she will give 80–90 cents back in human capital to her family, community, and country versus men's contribution of 30–40 cents on the dollar. Women have the power and influence to drive change.

| | |

However, women abdicate their power in many ways. Many are taught not to take up too much space, that they are not good financial stewards, that they can't have a family and a successful career, and that they should not "worry their pretty little heads" on advancing rights and healthy lives. But we *all* know that is not true. We have living role models every day that show us.

So, let us be bold. Let us have a discussion amongst women and men, fathers and mothers, daughters and sons, female and male coworkers about how we can change this dialogue to be healthier for all. This is not a women's issue but rather a place where women can take the lead on making change for all. Women have the power, and they can bring a healthy perspective to this dialogue about making change. With the support of men and women who want a healthier approach to financial well-being, together, we can forge a new path. It is time for us to change the lens of how we look at our lives. It is time for a new "money code of conduct." It is time for women to lead this battle for themselves and their families.

Here is what I know to be true. Change comes through study, habit, and relatable stories. Are you ready to learn through proper information and clarity of your own decisions? Do you want to learn better practices in multiple aspects of your life, including finances? Do you want to understand how the intersection of human capital and financial capital can be powered to achieve your life priorities? Do you want to learn how to align your values with your resources and your dreams?

I I I

This book will use a new and what I believe is a refreshing approach: It is called the "Lumination Approach." The definition of "lumination" from the Century Dictionary is "a lighting up; a flashing out. As of light or energy; an illuminating outburst." Lumination is the combination of the path to enlightenment around your journey, and a plan with connection to a community of like-minded and like-situation people and resources. In this approach, you will explore:

- What your money messages are and what your relationship is with money.
- You will learn how to unlock and diffuse your own financial "baggage" and open yourself to a new perspective.
- You will explore your values and the learning process that led to who you are today.
- You will explore six dimensions of your life: relationships, job/purpose, spirituality, play, health, and community.
- You will also learn what is working or not working.
- You will design your ideal life and how to connect it with your financial and human capital.
- You will learn how to address the triggers and potential barriers that get you off track.
- You will learn how to find the right coaches and strategists to assist you and your family along the way.
- With this strong base, you will be better prepared and more resilient to all that life can throw at you! Welcome to your "Lumination" journey.

"Don't live life in the past lane."

—Samantha Ettus

CHAPTER THREE

THE ONCOMING TSUNAMI OF WOMEN'S INFLUENCE

While not broadly understood, the influence of women on all of our lives is significant already and will only grow in its importance:

Women control over 50% of the wealth in this country or about $14 Trillion, and it is expected to increase to $22 trillion by 2022. Over the next 40 years, they are expected to inherit $28.7 trillion in intergenerational wealth transfers.[9] In fact, it is expected that women's wealth is growing by $5 trillion per year.

| | |

The fact that women also are outpacing men in college enrollment should result in an increase in the number of female senior executives and business owners, as well. Women are the primary breadwinners in 40% of U.S. households—but they are still remarkably underserved in the financial services industry: something like 51% of women with over a million dollars in assets don't have a financial advisor.[10]

- 85% of consumer spending is controlled by women.[11]
- 70% of major financial decisions are made by women.
- 80% of healthcare decisions are made by women.
- Women will be more focused on linking money to their goals, values, and priorities.[12] As we look to the future, women will change the faces of philanthropy and investment priorities, and ultimately help drive social change.

---

[9] Women and Investing Infographic 2019. New York Life. https://www.visualcapitalist.com/unlocking-power-women-investing/ (accessed August 6, 2020).

[10] Patsy Doerr, "Changing the Status Quo: How Women Are Leading the Charge on Impact Investing." Forbes. orbes.com/sites/patsydoerr/2018/10/23/changing-the-status-quo-how-women-are-leading-the-charge-on-impact-investing/#75cf22645bbe (accessed August 6, 2020).

[11] Michael J. Silverstein and Kate Sayre, *Women Want More: How to Capture Your Share of the World's Largest, Fastest-Growing Market.* Extracts. Boston Consulting Group. https://mkt-bcg-com-public-images.s3.amazonaws.com/public-pdfs/legacy-documents/file22016.pdf (accessed August 6, 2020).

[12] Women and Financial Wellness: Beyond the Bottom Line. Merrill Lynch/Bank of America. http://agewave.com/what-we-do/landmark-research-and-consulting/research-studies/women-and-financial-wellness/#top (accessed August 6, 2020).

- 65% of women say they want to invest in causes that matter to them.
- 84% of women say that understanding their finances is key to greater career flexibility.
- 77% of women say they see money in terms of what it can do for their families.
- 52% of women investors are interested in or currently engaged in impact investing, generating returns along with social returns.
- 90% of women surveyed indicated that they want to invest at least a portion of their wealth in a manner that aligns with their values. In addition, women are more inclined than the average investor to see their plans through to fruition.[13]

Forbes statistics show that women give away almost twice as much of their wealth as men (3.5% vs. 1.8%).[14] In fact, women give more than their male peers at virtually all income levels, even though women generally earn less, have less money in retirement than men, and have a higher life expectancy.

| | |

Despite the funding gap, startups founded and cofounded by women performed better over time, generating 10% more in cumulative

[13] Patsy Doer, "Changing the Status Quo: How Women Are Leading the Charge on Impact Investing." Forbes (October 23, 2018). https://www.forbes.com/sites/patsydoerr/2018/10/23/changing-the-status-quo-how-women-are-leading-the-charge-on-impact-investing/#53c9db1a5bbe (accessed August 6, 2020).

[14] Deborah Mesch, "The Gender Gap in Charitable Giving." Wall Street Journal (February 1, 2016). https://www.wsj.com/articles/the-gender-gap-in-charitable-giving-1454295689 (accessed August 6, 2020).

revenue over five years, according to the Boston Consulting Group (BCG).[15]

There are many more statistics that support the growing influence of women and their wealth. It is predicted that women will become the most influential force in all spending and investing decisions in this country. The tsunami is coming!

| | |

With this influence, women need a process in which they are more comfortable talking about their money and its potential impact. They need advisors who use a thoughtful, holistic, and comprehensive process to help them make informed and thoughtful decisions about how to accumulate, protect, and invest their resources in order to live the life they want for themselves and their families. The opportunity to fill this gap in advice and to introduce a process that is more appealing and tailored to the needs of women is significant.

Here is some of the evidence:

- Women are more likely to want to work with an advisor, but only 20% do.

---

[15] Allyson Kapin, "10 Stats That Build the Case for Investing in Women-Led Startups." Forbes (January 28, 2019). https://www.forbes.com/sites/allysonkapin/2019/01/28/10-stats-that-build-the-case-for-investing-in-women-led-startups/#1ae0390359d5 (accessed August 6, 2020).

- Over a third of women said that they had been patronized when dealing with the financial services industry.
- Most women are skeptical when meeting an advisor; again, 80% leave feeling misunderstood.
- 71% of women would switch advisors to someone who proactively makes managing their finances easier. They want someone who works around their schedule and lifestyle and provides information on how different lifestyle scenarios will affect their financial futures.

| | |

While the gender equilibrium of investing is changing, the ethos of investing is about to change drastically, but it has not happened yet. Women want life/wealth balance, i.e., they are time-strapped, want advisors who don't sell products, and are collaborative with other professionals to build their holistic life wellness plan.[16]

What does all this add up to at the end of the day? The financial services industry is missing out on $700 billion a year by not meeting the financial needs and expectations of women.[17]

| | |

How do advisors fill this disconnect?

---

[16] "Women, Investing, and the Pursuit of Wealth-Life Balance. PIMCO (September 2018). https://www.pimco.com/en-us/insights/viewpoints/women-investing-the-pursuit-of-wealth-life-balance (accessed August 6, 2020).

[17] "Serving Women as Financial Services Customers." Oliver Wyman. https://www.oliverwyman.com/our-expertise/insights/2019/nov/women-as-financial-services-customers.html (accessed August 6, 2020).

First, we need to change our money code, defined here as your money beliefs and behaviors, as well as how your money is or is not related to your values. Many of us need to shed the view that we do not have "enough" money or resources to qualify for good advisory partners. As a society, we must change the perspective by changing the way we talk, interact, and dialogue about money; this means we need to shift to a more substantive discussion of values, philosophy, and beliefs and away from comparisons to others and what they may have.

| | |

Second, we need to measure the value of ourselves (and the value of our advisors) in helping us reach our goals, hopes, and dreams. Typically, we are measuring against what others have or some random investment benchmark.

We need to believe that our best selves are developed by having hard, but vulnerable and truthful discussions as to what is important to us, rather than what we think may compare well or that "shows" well to others.

| | |

We must focus on meaning and connection with those we love and what brings us joy.

We must provide a safe environment for all to be truthful and open about our hopes and fears.

| | |

In my experience, this approach is more engaging with everyone, but most especially women. It helps build connections across generations. Overall, this approach leads to a healthier relationship with money by all.

The historical and more masculine perspective of money as a power to be accumulated is backward and outdated. We do not have to ascribe to this definition. Rather we need to see money as a gift that we can give (spend, donate, invest, direct) to achieve what we want for ourselves and those dear to us. We deserve the opportunity and the process to align money with our moral development.

PART II

REFLECTION: YOUR MONEY HISTORY, ROLE MODELS, AND VALUES

*"Owning our story can be hard but not nearly as
difficult as spending our lives running from it."*

—Brené Brown

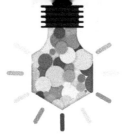

"Your mindset about money will actively create your own financial reality."

—Ann Sanfelippo

CHAPTER FOUR

YOUR MONEY CODE

We all have our own unique money journey. We develop our "money code" from the messages and activities that we have heard and experienced around money beginning when we are young children. This code creates the narrative in our minds that becomes the lens by which we view any financial decisions. Reflecting and acknowledging these messages is critical to having a healthy relationship with money and how it influences our self-esteem, our relationships, and, ultimately, our pursuit of purpose. These messages can help or hinder our financial decision making for years to come.

Many Americans avoid talking about finances even more than they avoid talking about sex and intimacy. The result is that we are facing

a crisis in financial literacy. Here are some statistics that help frame the issue:

| | |

- 63% of consumers could not correctly answer at least four out of five questions on a financial literacy quiz conducted by FINRA. These questions covered topics such as interest rates, inflation, bond prices, mortgages, and financial risk. This is up from 58% in 2009.[18]
- 1 in 6: The proportion of U.S. students who do not reach the baseline of financial literacy.[19]
- About one third of Americans pay just the minimum due on their credit card accounts each month.[20]
- 56% of consumers are concerned about running out of money in retirement.[21]
- Nearly 25% of Americans are not able to pay all their current month's bills on time.[22]
- Only 17 states require high school students to take a class in personal finance, a number that has not changed in four years.[23]

---

[18] National Financial Capability Study. Financial Industry Regulatory Authority. https://www.usfinancialcapability.org/ (accessed August 6, 2020).

[19] Financial Literacy and Economic Education Conference. Council for Economic Education, https://www.councilforeconed.org/events/conference/ (accessed August 6, 2020).

[20] Finra: Investment Education Foundation, National Financial Capability Study. https://www.usfinancialcapability.org/ (accessed August 6, 2020).

[21] Finra: Investment Education Foundation, National Financial Capability Study. https://www.usfinancialcapability.org/ (accessed August 6, 2020).

[22] Federal Reserve System. "Report on the Economic Well-being of US Households in 2016." https://www.federalreserve.gov/publications/files/2016-report-economic-well-being-us-households-201705.pdf (accessed August 6, 2020).

[23] Federal Reserve System. "Report on the Economic Well being of US Households in 2016." https://www.federalreserve.gov/publications/files/2016-report-economic-well-being-us-households-201705.pdf (accessed August 6, 2020).

Simply, our education system does not teach financial literacy. Further, most parents never received consistent messaging and values to develop appropriate behaviors to be role models for their children. If, as parents and adults, we do not educate ourselves on finances, then we perpetuate the cycle. While I believe the education system will figure out how to integrate this into the standard curriculum (and it may be years before that happens), we need to demonstrate ethical values and behavior by beginning the learning and teaching process in the home. We need to start the dialogue. Our children and we can learn from our own experiences and journeys. We can start by exploring our relationships and values around money. If we want to help this next generation, we need to be role models for the behaviors that we hope they develop.

| | |

Now begins your journaling, if you haven't started already. Please write your answers to these questions.

What are the money messages you have received? Think about your first memories of money discussions and activities. Did you have an allowance? Did you follow expected behaviors or do certain chores to earn that allowance? How did you access money or resources to make purchases? How old were you when you started to understand the value of money?

One of my early money memories was at 15 years old. My mom and I went to New York City and did what most visitors enjoy doing there. We went shopping, dined at a variety of restaurants, and went to the theater. When we came home, and my mom was going through the expenses with my father, he declared in front of me, "Lois, you can't spoil her like that. No man will ever be able to afford her." I was completely taken aback and asked, "Why do you think I won't be able to afford myself?" This began or perhaps reinforced my personal commitment to be financially independent.

| | |

Now, do not think badly of my father because he did over time give me the tools and knowledge to make good financial decisions. He gave me an allowance for the chores that I did around the house and forced me to pay for any nonessential items at a young age. In my teenage years, I had to research and pay for things like airline flights. Keep in mind, this was before the internet, so I had to call all the airlines and get prices and times of flights and then go back again to make the purchase. I was not given the option of a travel agent! This was a long and challenging process that I did not appreciate at the time. I thought he was mean and too hard on me because he forced me way out of my comfort zone. Later I would come to appreciate the fact that he forced me to come up with a process to get the information I needed, think of all the possible questions, and then budget accordingly. It was a fabulous lesson in that it helped me develop my financial decision-making skills and framework.

This process is called exposure therapy. It is the notion that you force yourself to do things that you are uncomfortable with but do them anyways. We do not see much of this modeling today in families or businesses because we are quick to rescue people or not give them the skills and tools to research and make informed decisions. Any experienced and successful professional or leader knows that we learn best when given a stretch opportunity even if we fail at stages or perhaps with the whole project. We learn best by taking risks and seeing the pros and cons of the decisions we make. Ultimately the only way to grow and learn new skills is by researching and doing things out of our comfort zone!

In the financial world, the consequences of bad habits and behaviors, with the risks taken knowingly or unknowingly, can be much more significant, and the ensuing emotional toll can also be even more significant. Contributing to our fears and stress are all the stories we read and hear about regarding fraud and financial manipulation. Financial posttraumatic syndrome disorder (FPTSD) is real. Many people have suffered through discrimination, a paucity of resources, fraud, financial abuse, and more. Divorce, widowhood, loss of a job, whether experienced directly or seen as a child, all affect our financial well-being. We may have watched our parents and other family members and friends experience these forms of loss. Our direct or indirect experiences can be very emotionally charged and create lasting memories and influence our relationship to money. Whether you have experienced the extreme or even had a mildly bad experience, your personal money code and behavior have been impacted in some way. We must explore these challenges and skills to move forward. As with most trauma, our bitter and negative feelings will likely continue to resurface at unexpected times!

I I I

Early in my career, I was an institutional equity (stock) trader. My job was to put together buyers and sellers of large blocks of stocks, typically between ten thousand to hundreds of thousands of shares. The payment came through as a commission per share of bought or sold stocks. I was hired on salary with the expectation that I would go to a variable compensation; this was the polite way of saying "commission." After four months, I was doing enough volume that, even on my worst weeks, I could still cover the rent. So, I set up a meeting with my boss and proposed that I was ready to leap from salary to a commission structure. He responded that I couldn't because the two men hired six months before my onboarding hadn't made the transition. He said it would be awkward if I transitioned before them. I was utterly bewildered because all our production numbers were posted, and they were doing as much as or more than me.

Shockingly, through discussions with my boss, I found that their salary was twice mine and that they had started with no more experience. I was emotionally crushed because I could not believe that just because I was a woman, I was paid half of what the men were making to do the same work. What added to my frustration and disbelief was that both these young men were given established and lucrative accounts. Conversely, I was expected to develop new relationships and accounts on my own initiative. Today, negotiating salary and benefits for women is a very touchy subject for me. This is just one of many stories in my journey that demonstrated gender discrimination in the workplace. Regardless, this is an important part of my money journey and affects me as much today as it did then.

| | |

After facing this blatant discrimination, I decided that I had to move from victim to advocate. My lack of information and trusting behavior allowed them to take advantage of me. No one would take my career as seriously as I did and still do. Now I have champions who help me to be bold. I needed to share this story and others that I have encountered to help motivate other women to see our reality. At the end of the day, we take our experiences and choose to be either a victim or to move forward as best as we can. I realized that I could be a change-agent against gender discrimination. I could also help other women to get the resources and information to be able to make better decisions than I did! We could, and can, ally with great labor and employment attorneys, human resource professionals, and financial advisors to collectively give women the information and grit to stand up for what is fair and deserved.

When I was at that same trading firm, I was never "given" the same established and lucrative accounts as my male peers. With the help of a female mentor, I decided to ask my boss if I could try to crack through on some of the larger firms that were not currently doing any business with us. What did he have to lose? We were not doing business with them anyway. He consented, and I began to work on building relationships. Quickly, I learned that the reason they were not doing business with us was they did not trust my peers or firm. Their biggest concern was that my peers would look out for themselves and our firm first, rather than placing the clients' interests first. Several went as far as to say they would never do business with me! As some know, I am resilient and tenacious. I spent time getting to know them personally and professionally, their history in the industry, their personal interests, and what made them really tick.

| | |

Over time, they started to trust me and gave me small amounts of business to test me. One client, Diane, specifically gave me a trade that required I protect her interests versus giving all the information openly to our full network. She wanted me to move in deliberate and incremental steps to execute the trade, hoping to get better pricing. It was a clear test. I chose what was right for her as the client and for her firm versus what was easy—the easy way being to get the trade done quickly and get my commission. Building Diane's trust in me resulted in her increased business with me.

But the story does not end there. Two years later, while I was on vacation, a senior trader in another office called Diane. He asked her if she would do more business with our firm if a senior male trader worked with her versus me, the junior woman. She thanked him for his offer and said she would think about it. Then she immediately called my boss and asked for a personal meeting. She stormed into his office and told him that the behavior of the other trader is exactly why she had not done business with our firm for all those years and that she would not do any business with that slimy snake! She would deal only with me.

I I I

While these stories are some that create very negative feelings around money and negotiating and fairness for me, I have others that have contributed to a more positive relationship with money. As a young girl, my first job was a paper route. I found I liked having a commitment that I was responsible for, and that earned me my own money. My next rewarding job was babysitting. I developed flyers and distributed them around the neighborhood. I quickly had more requests than I could manage. I loved earning money. I also loved being able to choose who were my favorite clients and to give them priority. That is a lesson that has stayed with me for most of my career: that a job is much more enjoyable when you work for, and with, people you like, trust, and enjoy!

Over the years, I have heard many money stories. My father and several of my friends have experienced the loss of their father at a young age. Often the surviving widow was kept in the dark about her resources for fear that, if she knew she had money, she would spend it all. From watching a loved one controlled by others and struggling with a feeling of helplessness because the information was not shared, the children often came into a career that earned them a good income and gave them financial skills. They never wanted to go through what they saw their mother go through. To them, it was not just the potential lack of resources that invoked change, but the lack of knowledge and trust around money that they never wanted to experience themselves. This was a hard lesson that clearly led them to develop more understanding and control over finances in their own lives.

I I I

I tell these stories to open your mind so that you can reflect on your own journey. All these money stories have shaped my relationship to money. Your stories have shaped your relationship and developed what is your "money code." What have been the money messages that you have received? Did you suppress any because they were painful? Did you watch a parent struggle after the loss of a spouse or partner to make ends meet? Did you struggle with school loans or racking up credit card debt?

Be assured we all have our own money baggage. The key is to explore it, change it, and accept that you may have chosen certain money behaviors or rejected others based on your journey. Are they reflective of what you want? Do you need to get someone to help you practice some new behaviors? If so, you are in good company.

| | |

Truthfully, we all need help, even financial professionals. Often, we are like the shoemaker who doesn't have time to make shoes for his children. The key is to find the coaches and relationships around you and begin to move toward a healthier financial fitness level.

You need to reflect on these stories to be able to move forward. Keep in mind that just because we have a broken part does not mean everything is broken. You cannot heal and develop a more positive relationship with money unless you have a process to immobilize that broken part and fix it. I will give you strategies to assist with this process and help you to develop healthier outcomes.

*"Everyone's got some greatness in them. You do. The girl
over there does. That guy on the left has some. But in order
to really mine it, you have to own it. You have to grab
hold of it. You have to believe it."*

—Shonda Rimes

CHAPTER FIVE

YOUR JOURNEY THROUGH
THE LUMINATION COMFORT ZONE

When I started my career, I wore suits from stores like Brooks
Brothers with bow ties and high-collared shirts. Not only
was this a terrible fashion look, but it symbolized a woman trying
to fit into a man's definition of business attire. Since then, we have
changed how we define work attire to reflect more femininity and
personality. We have found a way to express ourselves through our
attire, all while keeping things professional. We have indeed stopped
dressing to fit into a traditional male paradigm and embraced our
own style and flair. This is true for both women and men. We can
still look professional without looking like clones. Our dialogue
with money can follow a similar path. We can find our own voice
and our own expression of ourselves.

We all know that feeling when you put on a great outfit. It can change the way you feel about yourself and raise your confidence. You feel lighter, nimbler, and ready to take on the world. Our dialogue with money can follow a similar path. We can develop a new money persona and corresponding behaviors through awareness and intentional changes We can find our own voice and our own expression of ourselves.

| | |

That is what this process should feel like for you. Put on a new money look! Embrace who you are and what is unique and special about you and your situation, your values, and your priorities. Contemplate how everything that you do, you feel, you want, and you dream of is interrelated. Figure out how it incorporates all aspects of your life. Shine a light on what makes you feel better about yourself and where you are going. Stop talking about your net worth as though it's a clear picture of your self-worth.

How can money reduce stress versus creating it? Money should be the currency of choices that align with your values and priorities. Financial ownership should mean the independence to make informed decisions and choices rather than pressured or uninformed decisions.

| | |

To recognize the process and the different stages or zones that we go through in life and most certainly as it relates to money, I created the Lumination Comfort Zone. This evolution recognizes that due to our money history and the money messages that we received, we have developed our own personal money code or definitions around what success and failure look and feel like to us. Due to that training and messaging, we often start from the point of fear, a sense of not knowing or doing enough. This, in its broad definition, is the FEAR ZONE. When you see this chart, you will likely identify with some of the feelings and statements in that zone. As we research, explore, identify, and learn, we can begin to move forward on a clearer path. This is the LEARNING ZONE. In the last stage, we are acquiring skills, opinions based on good data or information, and that helps us to make good decisions, and this is the CONFIDENCE ZONE.

This model can be created for many things in life. Specifically, the Lumination Comfort Zone is focused on creating comfort around money and harnessing its power toward our goals and dreams. In our decision-making process around money, we need to accept where we are and what we need to do to move out of a "Fear Zone." We need to stop the guilt and shame over where we are in our plan. After all, this is just our starting point. Once identified and accepted, we can begin to learn and find a path to accomplish our priorities and goals. We also can begin to look for those who can help us in the process.

| | |

You will need true and trustworthy friends, coaches, and advisors in your developmental path. Often when starting a business or new project, we seek out advisors with different skill sets who will give us good candid advice. In this journey, you will need to again surround yourself with those positive influences who speak truthfully and share your best interests.

Are you familiar with the "Shine Theory?" It is a catchphrase that was coined by Aminatou Sow and Ann Friedman, who cohost a podcast, *Call Your Girlfriend*. The concept is that for women to have jealousy or compete with one another is pointless because when women collaborate, everyone shines. Thus, women who help other women by introducing them to people and resources that can help them are living that shine-forward concept. They are lighting the way for other women. Their collaboration and commitment to helping each other are powerful. As I hope you experience that help and advice, my hope is that you also think of ways that you can help women by shining a light for them.

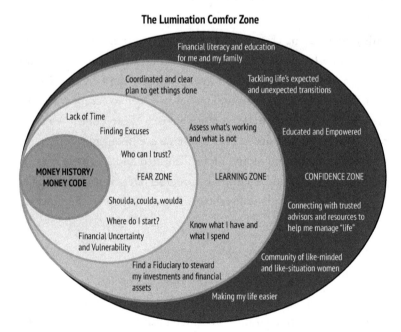

The Lumination Comfor Zone

I I I

Throughout this book, you will note the references to light, Lumination, transparency, and accountability to help you shine your
own light toward a more abundant and intentional life. Raising
awareness and understanding through the various tools and
exercises will hopefully teach you that you are not alone in this
journey. Intention comes from a deeper understanding of motivations and behaviors and consequences or results. To live your well
life, you will go through the process above and flex over time, pre-
dominantly between the last two zones as new knowledge arises.
Understanding where you are and what you need to keep moving
forward and through to the Confidence Zone will bring you peace
and security.

THE FEAR ZONE

"It's not the absence of fear, it's overcoming it.
Sometimes you've got to blast through
and have faith."

—Emma Watson

We begin with our money values and money messages that have shaped our own money journey. These are the messages that get embedded in our minds as to how we view and relate to money. These can include messages from parents or other influential people in our lives as to whether we were good at managing finances and money. These can include whether we felt that money was always tight or saw our parents having to save and be frugal, or on the other extreme, if we experienced that money was freely available for us to spend however and whenever we wanted. Further, if we had to "work" for our money, whether it was for an allowance or payment for jobs at a young age, this will influence our relationship to money and, therefore, our money values. All the messages, family influences, and work values are part of our individual money journey and influence our relationship today with money.

Typically, many people, and especially women, live in the Fear Zone. Here we are in that "shoulda, coulda, woulda" stage where we keep putting ourselves down for what we have not done. We also do not know where to start and perhaps are fearful of what we might learn. This is all very natural. In fact, almost every woman we have ever worked with finds herself here in the beginning. It is the nature of who we are, and we are quick to look at shortcomings versus what we have accomplished. Even if we are a CFO or CEO of a major business enterprise, we are more likely to focus on the "gap" in our accomplishments and progress than the "gain."

| | |

To get to the Lumination Comfort Zone, our first task is to address the fears, their source, and recognize that they are a bad habit that can be overcome with tools and skills. We have the power once we name our fears, own them, and develop a plan to overcome them. It is important to note that there is a difference between being cautious and being fearful. When we are fearful, we are frozen and unable to see our options. When we are cautious, we are protecting ourselves but still considering our next steps.

Every day we make choices around our priorities for the day. What do we want to accomplish for ourselves and for others? How can we best spend our time? What actions can we take that will make us feel good and have a lasting positive impact? What are the things we dread doing that suck time and energy from us? How do we prioritize the day? The best days are usually the result of planning. We gather information, prioritize, understand where we are, and think about where we need to get to achieve our goals. Usually, we have more to get done than we can possibly do in a day. So, we make choices. That is understandable. Some days, we are better at it than others. If you are an achiever, like me, the best days are when you get lots crossed off that to-do list! Regardless, we ultimately know that there is a defined process to get your to-do's done by listing them out, planning, prioritizing, and sometimes persevering through things that we don't necessarily enjoy or want to do but must get done. We manage time so that we can get the "what" (activities and chores) done based on our "why" (why I care to get this done).

What I know to be true is everyone has their own "baggage." If we hang on too tight to these issues and challenges, for fear of being vulnerable to criticism, we are unable to move forward. Rather we need to recognize that we all have our own issues that may not be pretty, but by being open and vulnerable, we can move through them. If we do not, we will stay in the Fear Zone. It is not healthy to be in the Fear Zone for any length of time because it wears us down and paralyzes us. It is critical we move to the Learning Zone quickly, and it is done by making some small, simple steps.

Perhaps a good perspective is to look at money the same way that we look at the resource of time. When we have much to do, we move forward by creating and prioritizing our to-do list and start moving through it; some of the tasks are easier than others. Some may be new tasks to us, but we break them down by identifying resources we need or series of smaller tasks. When we are at our best, we are allocating our tasks by the highest priorities to the lowest and determining where we can get our "highest and best use" of time. When we start a big project, we often begin in that Fear Zone of not knowing how to frame the project or how to start. Sometimes we find excuses because we fear exposing our vulnerabilities, such as lack of knowledge. But gradually, we figure out what we need in terms of outside resources and tools, and we develop a clear and organized plan.

Getting out of the Fear Zone takes time and reflection. You may revisit it from time to time, as well. That is all part of the process. The key is that through the exploration of our history and our fears, we begin to see other opportunities. We begin to see what we have learned along the way and what may be new possibilities that we never thought of previously. It is fluid and continual.

THE LEARNING ZONE

"I have learned over the years that when one's mind is made up, this diminishes fear; knowing what must be done does away with fear."

—Rosa Parks

The Learning Zone is not as frightening as most of us think it is going to be. In many cases, people find that their situation is not as bad as they initially thought. The unknown becomes known and we can begin to address our challenges and needs. In this chapter I will review the process. Later in the book, I will cover how to find the coach or advisory team to help you in this process.

| | |

The first step is to gather information. This includes your budget, expenses, and income. If this already seems daunting, there are several easy ways to do this. You can start by reviewing your bank account, credit card, and mortgage or rent statements to see how your money is being spent. Then you can gather your paystubs and the financial statements for your savings, investment, and retirement accounts. Often, it is helpful to review your last tax return to make sure you have all that you need to get a good sense of what is being earned or coming to you as income and what is being spent on living expenses as well as discretionary spending.

Ideally, you are earning more than you are spending, or at least are creating an awareness that you need to reduce spending to get on better footing. Having the information collected in order to review, itemize, and analyze is the big first step. Remember, while information makes you feel vulnerable, it is also a source of power to help you understand where you are and position you for a more in-depth exploration of where you want to be and how you might get there.

| | |

Over the years, in my work as an advisor and coach, I find that women are quick to judge themselves in both the Fear and Learning Zones. They often focus on self-deprecating statements such as "I haven't done enough" or "I don't have enough." Instead, appreciate that you have taken the steps to learn, to gain information to start the process of building your own choices, trade-offs, and priorities. That is enormous. It is like starting a new exercise program. You cannot be fit in a day. It takes steps, practice, discipline, measurement, and still, you have days where you backslide. But if you remain committed and disciplined, you can get in great shape, physically and figuratively, in your financial life. It is the same. It just takes some time, commitment, and focus.

Once you have your baseline, an accounting of what is being earned, and what is being spent, then you can begin to assess what is working and what isn't. Could you pay less in tax by saving more in your retirement plan (which likely wouldn't reduce your take-home pay that much)? It might increase both your retirement nest-egg and reduce your taxes! Are there things that sneak up on you, such as specialty coffees, which may be only $5 each but can amount to over $1,500 over the year and prevent you from affording other things that you value more? When I have done this analysis in the past, it is often the aggregation of what seems small, like ordering takeout from restaurants, that adds up to a much bigger expense than I realized.

| | |

Information gives us the power to reinforce or change our decisions and priorities.

THE CONFIDENCE ZONE

"Life is not easy for any of us. But what of that?
We must have perseverance and, above all,
confidence in ourselves. We must believe
we are gifted for something and
that this thing must be attained."

—Marie Curie

Once you have built your understanding of your current financial picture, you can move into the Confidence Zone. This step in the process is focused on what is essential in all aspects of your life and how you can build the best foundation to help you weather life's expected and unexpected transitions. Our paths are not a simple straight line. We face forks in the road, life choices and trade-offs, and sadly are often hit with unexpected changes and surprises that force us to pivot and change course.

In the Confidence Zone, you are building your financial literacy and education for you and your family. You are directed toward resources that will help you learn how to better align your resources with what you want in life. Because you are building this knowledge, your confidence around decisions is strong and often unwavering. In the best of circumstances, you also learn how to surround yourself with the right people to help you live this life. Hopefully, it is with good advisors. But perhaps most important, it is building a connection to your own community of like-minded and like-situation women—women who are also working to build an intentional prioritized plan for them and their family.

| | |

Later in the book, we will give you more tools for this process. That being said, the place where you want to live is the Confidence Zone. It is not a destination but a continual process of assessment, rediscovery, and realignment of priorities. There will always be changes and transitions in your life, and when you are in this Zone, you know how to focus the resources and strategies to work through them. The Comfort Zone is not about how much money you have in the bank. Instead, it is how you build an understanding to make informed and powerful choices around your money.

How do we see the intersection of this growing influence with the Lumination of our own money journey? Here I will tell two stories of how this process can dramatically change lives.

Theresa's Comfort Zone Story

Theresa and her college-age daughter, Caroline, were fighting over money (I bet you have never heard that before!) It was a typical fight, with the daughter spending more money than her mom thought was appropriate. Caroline was not keeping track of what she was spending, either. While Theresa did not specify what she felt was appropriate, she felt that Caroline was spending too much. The circle of disagreement went around and around. Caroline lived out of town, so I called her and said my goal was to get her and her mom to stop arguing about money. To do this, we were going to use an aggregating software program that uploaded her bank and credit card information. I went on to tell her that the software categorized expenses and that neither she nor her mom, were going to get everything they wanted. But at least this program would allow us all to have an informed dialogue. We got the data, and it was enlightening. The program helped build awareness of what was required to live in

Boston, where she goes to school. That was helpful for mom to see. In addition, there were some big *aha* moments for Caroline.

Awareness is the key here. Caroline began to see how all the little things added up. Most expenses were not significant, but in aggregate, they did seem excessive. Uber and Uber Eats were the biggest culprits sneaking up on her. We all want her to eat healthily and travel from place to place safely. Since the public transportation system was perfectly adequate to use during the daylight hours, we were able to reduce Caroline's travel expenses by 50%. By looking at each category, we were able to build a budget that Caroline thought she could live with while in Boston. We had dialogue around what would be the priorities for how she spent her money and what things she really did not care about that much about or could at least reduce. Caroline and Theresa stuck with the budget we came up with for a few months. Then Theresa increased Caroline's budget a bit based on the continued flow of information and a healthy dialogue between the two of them.

| | |

What is the best part of this story? By having information and being able to frame the dialogue about priorities and true needs versus wants, Theresa and Caroline could talk calmly and rationally about spending.

Information is power in this story because it allowed Caroline and Theresa the opportunity and framework of a healthy discussion. The best part is that now they have a better foundation to communicate and dramatically improve their relationship. So, by looking at the "what" and "why," the "what" was improving their relationship and the "why" was that they want to spend quality time together (not arguing). If we look at the "how" of the Lumination Comfort Zone process, we are able to put into motion a healthy framework to talk about money.

Effectively, we removed the unknown of what was needed, moving them to the Learning Zone. Over time gaining more data and information, they could move into the Confidence Zone, a healthier relationship with money and with one another, for both mother and daughter.

Michelle's Comfort Zone Story

Michelle's Comfort Zone story illustrates how the journey of learning and the ability to gain more control over her own money legacy can transform many lives. Thankfully, she took the time to develop her path. What a missed opportunity it would have been if she never claimed that power.

I I I

When I met Michelle, she was married to a domineering man who belittled her verbally, especially around any topic that involved money. Ironically, the source of their wealth as a couple and family was her family's business, which he had joined and led. When Michelle's husband passed away, she still didn't feel "ownership" of her financial resources, and therefore advisors took advantage of her in much the same way her husband did. They kept her in the dark and controlled all of the money decisions.

I had known Michelle for years. She asked me if I could have a meeting with her lead advisor because she was not feeling comfortable with her financial situation but could not pinpoint why. I agreed, and we set up a meeting with him and another associate of mine so that we could ask questions and learn from them both. The only problem was that Michelle never got to talk at that meeting. Her advisor talked over her and told us what he thought. We could tell by Michelle's body language that there was much more for us to learn about what she wanted. Perhaps, most important, it was clear that Michelle's advisor did not want our involvement, and we would later find out why. He was managing things to his benefit rather than hers. But that is not the focus of this part of the story.

| | |

To help us understand Michelle's money journey and what she wanted for her future, I asked if my partner Jim and I could sit in her living room, ask questions, and just talk. For an older person, in particular, as well as most of us, our living room is a much more comfortable place to have a conversation than an office. There was no agenda. We just wanted to ask questions and ensure that Michelle was in a comfortable and safe setting to answer them.

It was an enlightening afternoon. Michelle's advisor was pushing for her to move to Florida for the tax advantage. We uncovered that she did not want to live in Florida for several sound reasons. The most important reason was that at her mature age, her whole support network was in Cleveland. That was where she wanted to live, and the tax-driven decision did not make sense for her emotionally or in terms of her healthcare network.

| | |

During the next several hours, we learned what really had meaning for her and what she wanted for herself, her family, and her community.

We learned her fears and worries. Best of all, we explored her hopes and dreams. We did this not just once but many times, checking in on how she was feeling and ensuring she felt "heard." The key was to take the time and create a safe zone for her to open up, digest her thoughts and experiences, and be able to revisit them continually. This journey of discovery uncovered many ways to change her life for the better and to have her financial resources be more aligned around her values.

Once we understood her money history, goals, and priorities, we found a way to create her legacy, which was centered around life experiences and organizations that she cherished dearly. Since Michelle had financial resources, she had been solicited and gave to many disparate organizations out of guilt. By focusing her thinking around those organizations that she cherished and that had the biggest impact on her life, we developed a new focus on charitable giving to just three organizations. The plan meant she could dramatically impact those organizations in a way that had meaning. Michelle stopped making small, guilt-associated gifts. She finally recognized that she was making an impact on the organizations she felt most passionately about in terms of their mission and her experience with them over her lifetime.

| | |

After many discussions with her new and more engaged team of advisors, we married significant tax and estate planning strategies with large multiyear gifts. Michelle had a chance to be a steward of change and improvement at these institutions. She had a chance to change the lives of thousands of people in her community in a measurable way, and one that she could see in action in her lifetime. Perhaps the best day in my whole career, was when one of the institutions that Michelle donated to, which happened to be a women's school, shared with her the statements, pictures, videos, and letters of over 5,000 women who felt that their lives had been changed because of the women's leadership development program that Michelle had funded. To watch her live their stories, it just does not get any better than that.

In this case, Michelle had the means to make significant gifts. However, the point of the story is the journey that we all deserve when we think about our money. No matter if you have significant resources or not, if you focus your gifting on those organizations that align with your values and goals, you will feel good! It is this alignment that causes good feelings and knowing that you are giving to others in the most meaningful way that you can during your journey. It takes time to develop the path, as any journey should. Reflection and intention need to be revisited continually. The meaning of it all will come through your dedication to the process and the aligning of your time, or treasure, to the things that inspire you. Giving of yourself in this way is the true gift.

| | |

This story reminds me of the caterpillar building the cocoon so that they can break out and open into a new life. In order to renew, sometimes we need to reflect and reassess. We need to be still and build our safety zone for development. After that reflective period, we often should break open and shed a few beliefs, behaviors, and barriers to our own development. This process of the exploration called life is a cyclical living process and not necessarily a destination. We go through times and periods in our life where we will be in a "Fear Zone," not knowing the next step or process. We live more through exploring our vulnerabilities than just relying on our strengths or ability. When we are able to reflect and raise our awareness of what is needed or where there are gaps, we then can build a learning process. When we take the time and build a logical plan, identify who and what resources can help us, and trust them to be aligned with us, we can accomplish great progress, great change, and great goals. We move through a Learning Zone to build what we want, then make changes that help us to begin new behaviors and journeys. We can find comfort and confidence in the fact that we were thoughtful and aligned with our values, with our goals, and priorities. This is the Lumination Comfort Zone. It is a cycle that will repeat and illustrates a continual journey. Once out of the Fear Zone, we can easily live in a cycle between learning and building confidence around our next priorities and choices. It is a framework on which to build our own relationship with money.

The basic premise of existential philosophy is that you create who you are and who you want to be in life. You define yourself through three choices: by the stance you take, by what you avoid, and by how you work, love, and express your being in the world. Authenticity is taking responsibility for yourself as defined. So here we are, looking at Michelle's story. It is powerful because she changed her stance, she avoided small gifts that weren't making an impact, and she worked and expressed herself in the world by making a difference in the lives of her community. Through an intentional giving plan that included customized tax planning, estate planning, and smart investing, she was able to take control of her life and put in place a legacy that will last for generations.

| | |

It is not easy to change our view when every time we turn on a television or watch a sports or financial show, messages are sent that are reinforce the old paradigm. When we used to turn on channels like ESPN, coverage was focused on only winners and losers. We are now starting to see more life stories and deeper discovery through shows like "30 for 30," which humanizes the stories about athletes and sports. Similarly, we need to see less sensationalism in the news and financial markets coverage and shift toward a more human and story-rich approach. We need less fear and scare tactics and more stories about good human behavior. Throughout society, journalism, and media, we are beginning to see more coverage about positive change. Through this book and this process, my hope is to improve how we see ourselves and how we want to present our values and personality. Maybe it is just wishful thinking, but we can hope for a world where there is less "Wolf of Wall Street" and more organizations like The Gates Foundation who are making change by aligning values with their resources for good.

Choosing to take no new actions or steps is a choice to remain in a Fear Zone. Almost every story about an athlete or a great entrepreneur or philanthropist begins with their journey to build skills, knowledge, and strength to whatever capacity they are needed. They face challenges and failures and need to regroup and refocus. Similarly, the Lumination Comfort Zone is a continuous process of learning, revisiting, and building our money muscles. We can choose to be prisoners of our past or pioneers of our future. Face your fears. Everyone is or has been where you are now. Step into the new Zone. Step into the new you.

I I I

Did you know that if you have a written plan, you are 42% more likely to achieve your goals? Sharing our stories and intentions is a good first step. We are all on an emotional rollercoaster, especially as it relates to money. Fear around loss or lack of resources and knowledge is a real and powerful trigger. The key is to recognize it and try to take steps to build your own path to resilience. I cannot tell you that this journey will be easy. It is an area of life that is never easy, no matter how much money you have. However, the key is to reflect on your own money journey and money code. You will have hills to climb at several points in your life. But if you climb those hills, you will have moments of real joy as you prioritize and focus your resources around what makes you happiest. As I said, it will feel like a rollercoaster ride, but we must climb hills to get that thrilling ride on the other side.

*"If you think taking care of yourself is selfish,
change your mind. If you don't, you're simply
ducking your responsibilities."*

—Ann Richards

CHAPTER SIX

FINANCIAL FITNESS,
OR IS IT FINESSE?

In this chapter, we are going to connect how to build your personal resilience with the help you need to move through the Comfort Zones. In life, we need to work to develop skills in the areas we enjoy and feel strong, but also in those areas where we have weaker skills. We must build skills in our Learning Zone. The image of finesse has the skills that allow you to pursue a path but also to pivot when that path is not optimal. To have finesse, we must build our financial fitness.

What Is Financial Fitness?

Financial fitness is the process of building the skills and strength to weather the ups and downs that life throws at you. It is essentially the power of the freedom to have choices. Building your core strength in finances brings a sense of safety. You are building the skills to protect yourself in tough times or when things go wrong or just not how you planned. Financial fitness opens you to taking advantage of opportunities that present themselves at expected and unexpected times.

The Four Pillars of Financial Fitness

Balance

- The ability to adjust or change course.
- The capacity to respond to the unexpected in a disciplined and thoughtful way, understanding the pros and cons of choices.
- Brings agility so that you can pivot without stumbling, because your body and mind can adapt, and knowing you can correct your balance and avoid falling.

Stamina

- Building endurance and vitality.
- Living life to its fullest and knowing you have choices about what you can physically do.
- Enjoying family and friends, an encore career, travel.

Flexibility

- The freedom to make choices, stretch options.
- The ability to adapt to the expected and unexpected.
- The opposite is rigidity, pain, limitations, and insecurity.

Strength

Strong core, good bone density, supports movements and functions.

- Builds over time and involves repetition of good form and exercises of mind and body.
- Gets you through tough times with grit and resilience.

When our son was young, he was good at many sports, and we let him play everything. Several coaches wanted him to focus on only their sport, but I remember our pediatrician explaining that for better body, bone, ligament, and muscle development, it was best for kids to play multiple sports. If they focused too heavily on one sport, the overuse of those muscles and ligaments could lead to more injuries.

I I I

Our lives are very similar. If we focus on just one aspect or just one area of financial fitness, we lose out on the development of others, often causing problems down the road. We must focus and build all four pillars in our financial lives to have true financial fitness.

For purposes of our process, financial fitness leads to financial wellness, which is a balanced approach to exploration, understanding, and skill development. Financial wellness is a documented plan to align your values to your hopes and dreams in the six areas of life: Relationships, Job/Purpose, Spirituality, Play, Health, and Community. This is accomplished by using your human capital and financial capital in an intentional way. It is an active living process, not a destination. Life does interfere, despite our best intentions and plans. So, it does need to be adjusted for the expected and the unexpected.

| | |

Like many other things in life, especially time, whenever you say "yes" to something involving money, you are saying "no" to something else. When we do not prioritize, we could be unknowingly saying "yes" to things that have less meaning or are harmful, resulting in us not having the resources for things that have more meaning. Similarly, if you avoided working on a healthy lifestyle and going to the doctor for a "check-up," you might be unknowingly contributing to your own poor or declining health. We must be proactive. It is critical that we pour our energy into defining which things deserve our most precious resources: time, and money. Putting yourself last can be literally life threatening.

"If you don't like the way your kids are behaving, hold up the mirror."

—Jeff Ettinger,
husband of the author

CHAPTER SEVEN

VALUES ARE CAUGHT, NOT TAUGHT

A Historical Perspective

In this chapter, we are going to look at what your values are and how you saw, caught, tested, and eventually developed your own set of core values. As we begin to move from our understanding of how to build our Comfort Zone, we have to understand that our "why" on any given day are those values we hold dear today.

Our "why" is developed from our values and becomes our purpose, our reason to have our feet hit the floor every day and move forward.

Our values should be at the core of our actions. Sometimes our actions are not aligned, and this chapter will help you reflect and perhaps refocus on those values. This may also give you a chance to reflect–if you are a parent, aunt, uncle, or grandparent—what values you hope are "caught" by those whom you mentor and act as a role model.

| | |

When our kids had their own budgets, they learned how to prioritize. They also learned responsibility for their decisions. As a parent, it is easy to want to "rescue" our children. Our oldest daughter, Emily, has always been a wise old soul in the body of a girl, and now a young woman. She often teaches me as much as I teach her.

When Emily was in high school, we started her on a budget that would pay for all her purchases, including toiletries, clothing, tickets to dances and events, etc. This is when iTunes was first becoming popular. After about six months, she went over her budget, downloading 99-cent songs from Apple. She was horrified that she had not realized that all the small purchases would add up as quickly as they did. That was the first good lesson: that when small purchases go unmonitored and uncontrolled, it can add up to a very large expense.

The second lesson was about how to fix the problem. Emily's mistake cost $20, and it became a fabulous learning experience for us. We were able to talk through what happened and what she could do differently going forward. She had to work her way out of the mistake of spending more money than she had by cutting back during the next several months. Perhaps the best silver lining, as parents, was that this relatively small mistake of $20 happened while she lived with us instead of it being a bigger mistake, like the $2,000-plus debts that many college kids rack up.

| | |

Many people do not realize that college kids get lots of credit card offers even though they have no current earnings, and thus no way to pay the debt off. Clearly, having a teachable moment of $20, while humiliating to our typically responsible child, was a lot better than, making a much bigger mistake later. Emily now knows to charge only what you *know* you can pay off.

A few years later, her iPod broke. This was a favorite item since she loved music. I tried to rescue her by giving her money to replace it. Emily refused my offer and said that she was proud that she was managing her finance without our help! As such, she thought she could have enough saved in a few months to purchase a new one. I realized the best thing I could do was to let her control her money decisions and not rescue her, as that would send a very mixed message. Truthfully, I think she was the teacher in this case, not me!

Your Values Journey

Now to learn more about what has influenced your values, there are a few additional exercises for you. Grab your journal and begin.

Heroes Exercise

Name three people, known or unknown to others, who are your heroes. What are the attributes or characteristics that you most admire?

| | |

Name three people in your immediate community whom you admired, worshipped, or idolized while growing up. These could be teachers, coaches, parents, other family members, or friends. What are two or three characteristics that caused your admiration or idolization?

Now write down what you like about yourself.

| | |

Compare these lists. What attributes are in your heroes, and those that you most admired, that are also in you? Do you find it surprising that you have these characteristics? Take a minute to let that soak in.

If you are like most women, you spend a lot of time talking and thinking about what you want to improve upon or change in yourself. Stop shorting yourself. This is the time to let it soak in that you do have characteristics that you admire, based upon who you have admired in your life, as a child, and through adulthood. That is a good thing!

Bullies and Bums Exercise

Were there people, family members, or community members that bullied or caused you to have bad feelings about yourself? What did they do, or perhaps not do, that brought on these negative feelings? What feelings did those activities generate for you? How did you respond?

| | |

Many of us have been bullied or manipulated at some point in our lives. Often, it is someone who is close to us, i.e., a family member, coworker, or someone in our inner circle, who is the bully. Sadly, we often cannot just dismiss them and cut them out of our lives.

Personally, I have a family member who bullied me for years. It is well disguised at times, and it is hurtful. Yet, for decades, I let it go on because I just could not believe that family would do this to me. I was in a perpetual cycle of giving him the benefit of the doubt and believing there had to be decent intentions that I just did not see.

| | |

Finally, I requested a joint counseling session to help us get through our challenging relationship and for the good of our extended family. During a counseling session, his bad behavior and bullying occurred, and my feelings were validated. While this did not change his behavior, what I needed was for an independent party to see his bullying and my corresponding backing down to a point of weakness. Why I allowed this to go on for so long is a mystery. However, having a professional see it as it was happening helped me to move on.

I still do not manage this dynamic as effectively as I would like to, but I can compartmentalize the interaction better than I did previously. I also am better at seeking coaching and advice when I do have to prepare to deal with him. Yes, I do have to prepare for our interactions so that I do not fall back into the victim's behavior and allow myself to be hurt. While I am not great at it, I am better at managing our interactions and limiting how vulnerable I make myself.

| | |

I tell this story because we all have people who make us feel like a failure. As we think about the values we have, we must look at what we admire, but also what makes us vulnerable. If we have been bullied or someone made us feel bad about ourselves, we need to do the work to understand that we can let go of that one person's opinion or action. One person cannot define us.

Over time if we work at it, we can use this bullying experience to develop our strength. The process begins with the recognition of why you react negatively. Bullies are master manipulators. They can spin anything into a barbed comment or action that is wounding to you. Your history with a bully can build strength of character as you determine never to be that type of person to others. You might be more empathetic, communicative, sensitive, or understanding because you did not feel any of those qualities in that bully.

| | |

Reflecting on this and perhaps other things that generate bad feelings for you, what are the three to five behaviors that you just cannot tolerate because they violate your core values? As a result of knowing what can "set you off," what would you now list as your three to five core values?

Write a Letter to Money

Using these values and what you learned in the previous chapter, now write a letter to "Money" as if it were a person. What makes you feel "rich" in this definition? Who and what is important in this letter? Try to be succinct and focused on the values and how they relate to the six areas of life. What do you really want? Tell this person, "Dear Money," what you want for them.

Bullies and heroes are both a part of your journey. Taking time to reflect on their behaviors and values and what you have taken away from those relationships or changed in your behaviors and values at your core are critical elements of your Lumination journey.

Secondly, you have "caught" values from how you were raised. Have you decided to hold true to those same values or do you pivot based on your own priorities and beliefs? There is no right answer. It is just part of your evolution and exploration of what you value and prioritize.

| | |

Taking that further, think about your role as a parent, leader, family member, and friend. Who looks to you to be a role model?

PART III

THE BUILDING BLOCKS

In the previous section, you explored through various lenses and exercises how your personal experiences and relationships have created a money journey that impacts your values and priorities today.

The next section will explore how to build on that knowledge the foundational building blocks for your future, in which you live a more intentional and abundant life. In this section, we will explore a multidimensional approach to financial wellness. Building financial fitness is like building physical fitness. It requires a comprehensive approach to strength, balance, flexibility, and endurance. Whether we are an artist, musician, entrepreneur, athlete, or writer, a balanced and intentional approach to creating our path for success is needed.

"You are the one that possesses the keys to your being. You carry the passport to your own happiness."

—Diane von Furstenberg

CHAPTER EIGHT

UNDERSTANDING YOUR ENERGY SOURCES

The Four Energy Fields in Your Life

What creates or reduces your energy comes from four different sources. Understanding the impact of all four will help you to use them as a source of strength in your Lumination process. You can increase performance and focus by managing these areas effectively. They can also provide resilience and renewal. To help in your journey, you will need to reflect on how effectively you use these energy sources.

Physical Energy = Physical Strength
Requires Periods of Building Followed by Rest

Have you ever noticed how a workout gives you more energy after-ward, not less? As an ice hockey player, I come home at night after a game and cannot settle in for bed for a few hours! Often, I spent the hour before my game thinking I do not have the energy to play because I am too tired. It is always surprising that even when you dread a workout because you are exhausted, you come out feeling better and more energized.

As you build physical strength, it is important that you realize you need to work hard to build each muscle group. To gain and reach higher levels, you must rest in between to give your body a chance to restore and prepare for the next round. This becomes important as we think about any challenge that is physically (and mentally) taxing. We do have to take breaks and rest in between periods of hard work.

| | |

When I broke my ankle playing hockey, I was determined to recover as quickly as possible, and I tried to do more than the physical therapist recommended. I thought that if I did more, that would mean I would heal faster and get better faster. My doctor and therapist explained to me that pushing too hard before your body is ready can do more damage than good. It was a good reminder that more is not always better. Following a disciplined process of building followed by resting is much better for our bodies and our minds.

I find it interesting that starting a new sport, workout, or challenge is often frustrating and difficult when we begin. We cannot get into optimal shape and skill development without a clear plan. We need to build from where we are beginning and identifying milestones that we need to accomplish before moving to the next level. As we build strength or basic skills, we then feel more physical strength and power.

| | |

A few years ago, a friend who is a personal trainer was shocked that I did not do chin-ups or pull-ups in my workout regime. Gauntlet thrown down! I committed to doing them. Shockingly, despite some pretty good upper body strength, in my first attempt, I could do only two! But over the coming months, I challenged myself to build up to 10–12 repetitions during my workout. Interestingly, it built not only my upper-body strength but also my core abdominal and back strength. Like many goals, there was more benefit than I originally expected. It feels great to accomplish this type of self-challenge, such as reaching a physical goal. A sense of power comes from knowing a milestone was achieved, but also from knowing our body is more resilient and balanced. It prepares us for endurance through future challenges.

Knowing that physical activity can be a source of energy, next time you hit a wall at work or are working at a disastrous project, go for a walk, hydrate, and take care of your body. Have you ever noticed that when you are outside exercising without distractions that you often have those *aha* moments when you solve problems or have great ideas? Physical activity and strength are related to our development and success in all areas of life. This is true when we are young and nimble, as well as when we age and become more limited. We must define what can help us build that physical strength and energy at an appropriate level for where we are in life. We need it at every stage of life to give us more energy, focus, and drive.

Emotional Energy = Emotional Flexibility
*Build an Emotional Response That Is Appropriate
to the Event and Manageable*

When we are in a threatening situation, perceived or real, we need emotional flexibility to help us experience not only fear, but the curiosity and resiliency to surmount the obstacle. If we have good emotional energy, we can find the positive and motivate ourselves to go through a process toward a positive purpose. Similarly, we derive emotional energy from doing things we enjoy and find relaxing. For me, those would include outdoor activities, listening to music, reading, or spending time with those I love. Where does your emotional energy come from, exactly?

Every year I go on an annual girl's ski trip with the same group of friends. While we do love to ski, we would all tell you that four days of being together filled with laughter, love, and connection is what rejuvenates us on many levels. Those emotions are contagious and healthy for our brains and bodies. We talk about multitudes of topics and interests. Our brains are stretched and connected with each other through sharing, freedom to say anything, exploring new thoughts and boundaries, and simply experiencing the joy of laughter and humor. What has been most telling is that when we have returned from those trips, at least one of us has made significant changes in our lives to get to a healthier place professionally or personally. Sometimes the change was in an area that we had not even discussed! However, getting our brains into a positive emotional state opened us to making changes and exploring new horizons and opportunities. Good friends can be the greatest fountain of positive emotional energy.

| | |

We often are faster to recognize emotional energy that is unbridled and leads to outbursts. Things happen, and our first impulse may be very inappropriate. A better process is to take time to reflect on the emotions that are created in these circumstances and that we recognize whether they are real, or we are throwing a bit of our own fabricated kerosene on them to ignite even more fire. Sometimes we create a bit more story than is true.

I am a big fan of the 24-hour rule, which sometimes I need to extend to 48 hours to better manage my emotions to a thoughtful and reasonable place and response. If you do not know this rule, it is to wait at least 24 hours after an incident, email, or instigating issue that evokes a big emotional reaction for you before you respond. The theory is that often our initial reaction is overblown and will be something we will regret later. After 24 to 48 hours, we can be more thoughtful, or more empathetic to what might have caused or brought on that reaction. We can then provide a more measured and appropriate response.

| | |

As someone who can get emotional, I often use this time to talk to friends and family who will help me to frame the issue better and see multiple perspectives. The bottom line is that emotional energy is critical but also can be the most explosive and unbridled areas of energy. If not well managed, it can be harmful. If our energy is well managed, it can be very powerful and constructive.

Mental Energy = Building Mental Strength
*Realistic Optimism Helps Us to Keep Sight
on Our Target When Things Go Awry!*

Mental energy gives us the opportunity to learn from mistakes and to be open to mental resiliency. Did you know that creativity requires both hemispheres of the brain? The left is the logical, linear thinking, and the right is the more visual, big picture side. We need both sides of our brain to be effective, and sometimes we need to really refocus on stimulations for both. At work, mundane tasks can overwork the left hemisphere. We must make time for the right hemisphere. Both sides need a chance! For some of us, if the right side feels caged, we are even less productive with the left side.

A tool that I use is to keep my favorite creative outlets close by, especially in long meetings and planning sessions. Some tools that I use are coloring books, puzzles, putty, or magnetic manipulating toys. Yes, I encourage things like this in meetings because it helps keep that creative right side stimulated when we are often working through less creative tasks. In our offices, we often have puzzles or other creative challenges on top of our file cabinets so that our team members can take a break and get their mental energy recharged.

| | |

Reflection is our "renew" strategy with mental energy. Often, we do not take this time. As leaders, we should encourage ourselves and others to take "clarity breaks." What is surprising is that the best way to do this is to have a pad of paper and a pen and a quiet space and time just to think and reflect. The idea is to let your mind take you wherever it wants to go. You do not need props or expectations. All you need is time, and you will discover what pops up in your mind.

Mental energy can also be recharged by walking or exercising, listening to music, exploring art, and other creative forms. Try to use these simple methods in your daily routine for "mental energy" breaks, and you will find that you have better and more creative ideas, and more energy and focus on your required tasks and projects. Just like the dog that gets up and does a good stretch, moves to a new toy, or explores their surroundings, we need to find ways to give our right hemisphere a chance to stretch. We need to give our minds time to refresh and renew. It is likely, though, that your mind will refocus after a long period of grinding. Stretching our minds is sometimes best done with simple breaks and a change to a creative outlet.

Spiritual Energy = Our Source of Motivation and Drive
Commit to Benefiting Others as Well as Ourselves

Empathetic people are those who are good at walking in the shoes of others and understanding their needs and wants. They often have more daily motivation. They are driven by a higher purpose than simply serving themselves. A good example is that if you smoke or drink, it is much easier to quit when you are pregnant because you are looking out for the baby versus just yourself. As we embrace change, Five percent of our behavior is consciously focused on intentional behavior or change. Shockingly 95% of our behavior is out of habit and is an automatic response or action. We have learned that it takes from 30 to 60 days to develop a new habit and, unfortunately, just a few days to fall back to old habits. Change needs to be moderate and incorporated into a thoughtful and manageable process.

| | |

In the past few years, I have experienced the benefits of mindfulness at work. To get started, I began meditating one minute a day; yes, that may seem wimpy to you, but I needed to start slow and build. Then I went to 3, 5, and 10 minutes overtime. By building slowly, the change was manageable, and it was a modest change that I could accomplish.

Truthfully, if the first step were to go to 10 minutes, I do not think I would have sustained the process and been successful. It would be too easy just to skip it because I did not have enough time. By gradually increasing the time, I could build what worked for me and what I liked in a way that could become a habit. I think everyone who has achieved this goal can feel the benefits of meditating. I am still too tightly wound, but I manage myself better! It is a work in progress, but I can honestly say it has helped me to gradually appreciate the benefits because each new level felt like a big accomplishment and brought positive results!

| | |

Our spiritual energy needs to be built and maintained and is likely the area of our lives that is most underdeveloped and ignored. Great energy can be built from reflecting on how we can be better for and to ourselves, and for and to others. While guided meditation helps me because I need the coaching, everyone can find their own path. The key is to take the time to reflect on your spiritual energy and how to build it. Without it, you can be so busy doing that you do not take time to really appreciate and focus on the meaning of your choices and actions. Without reflection, you are often less sensitive, more hurtful, and less of a friend or person than you want to be in life. With mindful, spiritual energy work, you can live a more fulfilled and rewarding life.

As a person who has historically been quicker to act than to be reflective, I have a great reminder on my desk at work. Several years ago, my best friend, Pat, and my business partner, Ken, were in the same Leadership Cleveland class. They spent at least one day per month together learning about different inner workings in the City of Cleveland. However, since they both are pranksters, they took this opportunity to think up activities that would bring a good chuckle at my expense.

| | |

One day they both showed up in my office with a gift. It was a pair of pink brake pedals in a Lucite box with an accompanying pledge that I had to sign to show my commitment. To formalize my commitment to slowing down via STOP (**S**top, **T**hink, **O**bserve, **P**roceed) they brought in our company compliance officer to notarize the document! Below is the document for your entertainment.

I, Heather Ettinger, will use my new brakes as a daily reminder to:

I promise Ken and Pat—my new brain mechanics—that I will make thoughtful decisions on my time and resources with the exception of:

1) Family
2) Any and most of Ken Requests
3) Any and all of Pat Requests

I will slow down and hit the brakes when I need to take a BREAK or whenever Ken and or Pat tell me to.

　　　　Jeff can trump all stop and go lights at any time.

　　　　Accepted: _____　date: _____

| | |

I did not miss the point of this exercise. The formal document combined with the pink brake pedals created a humorous reminder of my commitment to slowing down! However, my actions sometimes deviate from that path because I do not stop and reflect. Now I have a visual reminder every day in my declaration and my "brake" pedals. If I am intentional in what brings me joy and focus on those people, things, and activities, then I am happier and have more energy. The purpose of this chapter is to help you remember that you need all four areas of strength building—physical, emotional, mental, and spiritual energy—to take on the Lumination process.

Now we will explore these four areas in your life and what adds to or depletes these resources. In your journal, you can create your own diagram.

The Four Energy Fields:
Physical • Emotional • Mental • Spiritual

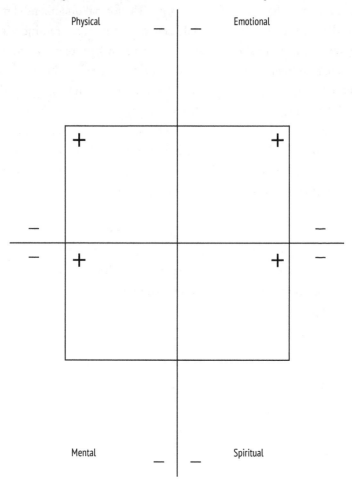

Build a four-quadrant grid. The four quadrants are the four energy fields. The inner box of the four quadrants is the positive and more controllable intentions. The area outside of the box represents the negative and often more uncontrollable elements. Write in the outside areas of the four quadrants the negative sources of stress, or those things that you do not control that affect your energy.

| | |

In each quadrant, write in the "+" inner box the things you do or would like to do to build energy in that area of your life.

In each quadrant, write in the outer box the behaviors, people, or activities that are unconstructive or destructive in each area.

| | |

You will need to look at all these aspects of your life, sources, and detractions, to move forward as you do some of the hard work. What things can you easily build into your days to improve your energy fields?

I filled out a sample below. Even as an overachiever, I try to be reasonable and focus on one, two, or three things at most in each area. You might want to revisit this grid in six months to see if you are staying true to your plan. If you are not, maybe it needs to be posted somewhere where the reminders are more visible! Give yourself permission at each stage to renew and reflect on each area. Try to have several things that bring positive energy in each area. While this may take some time, it is important to have a balance of resources.

| | |

Here is a sample to help guide you.

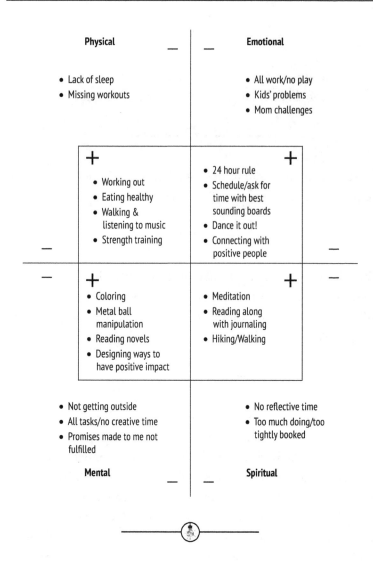

Awareness of what builds or sucks out our energy is important to recognize before we move on to talk about our intentional plans. This is not a quick, short process, but an evolution. At times you will need to focus on creating energy to fill your voids. Now you know some of the tools to add to those things that rejuvenate you.

"Life is not measured by the number of breaths we take, but by the moments that take our breath away."

—Maya Angelou

CHAPTER NINE

THE PILLARS OF LIFE, HEALTH, AND WELLNESS

Defining the Building Blocks

In the last chapter, we looked at what created or drained our energy in the physical, emotional, mental, and spiritual areas of our life. Now we will look at these pillars as if they related directly to our comprehensive development. Several years ago, I had the good fortune of going to Canyon Ranch and learning about their four pillars of leading a healthy and strong life. Often, we are good in maybe one, two, or three of these areas but rarely all four. The only way to get the healthiest life that is physically, emotionally, mentally, and spiritually connected is to build all four areas intentionally. Each one requires its own plan to cultivate healthy behaviors and practices. I use physical references here, just like a personal trainer would if you had a comprehensive fitness plan. Since we are talking about financial fitness, this analogy can be very helpful.

The emotional building block is balance. It is the capacity to adjust and respond to the unexpected in an even and thoughtful way. Positive feelings in this area come from a feeling of equity, harmony, and being centered. Emotional balance comes from being able to pivot or readjust without losing your balance, and "falling over." You are striving to have a balance of several things rather than too much of too few things. Having a balance of activities brings emotional joy and stability.

| | |

The physical building block is strength. What makes you strong or weak? Bone density comes from strength training, just like core strength is necessary to support every other action of your body. You need to have the physical strength to help power you through adversity and challenge. When you ignore strength training, you can suffer injuries, and typically experience more body aches and pains and sickness. You must train to build strength and be both consistent and persistent. But when you have it, your body can support you through change.

The intellectual building block is mental endurance. This is your source of: vitality, intensity, pizzazz, zest, drive, vigor, and mental stamina. Understanding the reasons, research, the "why" to your behaviors and activities creates mental fortitude. We need to think about why we eat well, why we exercise, why we want good health. It is all to give us the mental strength to take advantage of opportunities, and to push through to be active and make good choices on those days when we have less drive or resilience.

| | |

The spiritual building block is flexibility. This is derived from agility, the ability to change, and be open to difference. When we are rigid, we have more pain, both physically and emotionally. Conversely, by building grit and resistance, we can recoil and maneuver through the twists and turns of life. Working on flexibility helps us to keep our bodies and minds safe from injury. Mindfulness and meditation are often exercises that help us build spiritual flexibility.

Framework: Finding the Courage to Be True to Yourself

The natural response of all of us is to focus on those areas that come easiest. However, it is important to build all these areas in your life plan. If you hired a life trainer, just like if you hired a personal physical trainer, they would create a plan that included all these areas. You would need balance, strength, endurance, and flexibility. Some areas are much harder than others, but it is important to spend time developing all of them to build true resilience.

The key to success is to take the time to reflect on your values and how each challenge and opportunity fits into these four categories. To help you explore how to use this in your own life, I will share some challenges and how reflecting through this lens helped me to stay true to my values and find a path that worked for me.

| | |

When I first had children, I was also juggling a significant career. I found that I could be out every night of the week at a business event. However, my family was my priority. Feeling the pressure of work, I would say yes to too many events and not be home as much as I wanted to be. So, I used this four-step perspective to help me develop the plan to accomplish what I wanted (rather than doing what I thought others wanted me to do, and being miserable as a result.)

The first step was that emotionally I needed more balance. I wanted to be home at least two of the four weekday nights (Monday–Thursday) with my family. I loved my job, but my emotional energy also came from being a good partner, mom, and active participant in family life. This is not an easy course of action, but I also know that downtime and connecting with my family gave me an emotional lift. Seeing their development was a journey that I wanted to be present for and not miss. I also personally needed time with them and my husband. Home was my safe place where I am surrounded by those who love and support me the most.

| | |

Part of my process included intellectual analysis. I reflected on the fact that while being at business events was good, I really did not need to be at all of them. First, I needed to think about what the priority for me and my company was overall. What were the essential visibility needs of the firm, and what would my role be in developing those? It was and is important for me to be seen in the community and develop those business relationships, but I also needed to prioritize where I had to be and where I might want to be. It came down to focusing on the quality of the event and time spent versus quantity of events. Interestingly, time poorly spent, meaning where I don't feel as if I am making a difference or impact, drains me. Conversely, time well spent energizes me.

On the other side, I needed to ensure that I was at the most important events for my kids. What proactive steps could I take to plan for all those events? For our first meeting with teachers and coaches, I would ask for calendars, dates, potential dates, the timing of events during the previous year, etc. I tried to block my calendar out to prevent conflicts. My husband used to tell teachers, "You cannot give Heather a date too far in advance, even if it is not confirmed!" Being proactive helped reduce the number of conflicts and reduced my stress!

| | |

The next step might have been the hardest: practicing saying no without feeling guilty! I literally had to develop the physical strength to say no. That may sound trivial, but I needed to build my core power to say the word without hesitation. I struggle with guilt and the feeling that I am letting others down. My expectations of myself and what I can commit to are sometimes way too high. To get better at not feeling guilty and not giving in to unhealthy pressure, I had to convey with the right words and unwavering strength that this was what was best for my family and me. I rehearsed, saying things like, "What a great invitation. I am so sorry, but I am already booked two nights that week, and I need to be home that evening. Please know that I think your event is important. I wish that I could be there, but I will have to wait until next time. I need to be home for my family and me." Most people, or certainly the ones who are aligned with my values, supported and truthfully admired me more for having conviction and intention around my priorities.

The last step is spiritually feeling at peace with my decision and knowing when I did need to be more flexible. When our second daughter was diagnosed with ADHD, the doctors and therapists coached us to be aware of how my stress and running at a hectic pace negatively affected her. I am very thankful for that lesson, as I do not think it is just for ADHD kids. When we are stressed, we project stress on others, or at least I do, and it needs to be better managed. Sometimes someone else's sense of urgency is not our own sense of urgency. As mentioned earlier, a great tool to ensure a thoughtful and appropriate alignment of my actions with my priorities is to take 24–48 hours before giving an answer to invitations and requests. Sometimes the quick response to what I think I want to do—or what I perceive others want me to do—is not what ultimately is going to make me happy. Having that chance to reflect and be flexible helps me make better decisions.

PART IV

ASSESSING YOUR INFLUENCERS AND INFLUENCES ON THE SIX AREAS OF YOUR LIFE

"I've come to believe that each of us has a personal calling that's as unique as a fingerprint—and that the best way to succeed is to discover what you love and then find a way to offer it to others in the form of service, working hard, and also allowing the energy of the universe to lead you."

—Oprah Winfrey

CHAPTER TEN

THE SIX AREAS OF LIFE

You are unique! Your journey is unique too: past, present, and future. To design your intentional life and truly live it in your future, you will need to spend time thinking about what is important to you. Again, there will be some reflection back on what has influenced you in the six areas of life and how you want to carry that forward or how you will cease to be constricted by the past. You will want to be open to thinking in new ways and truly pursuing what you love.

For all of us, the focus of our daily lives falls neatly into six areas. Not all areas are equally important—that is part of what makes you unique. Only you can truly assess how much time and energy you want to put into each area, based on its meaning to you and your family. As you go through the exercises in this next section, continue to use a notebook or clean paper to take your notes and draw the diagrams. You will quickly see how interrelated these areas can be in your life. However, to start this exercise and to get the benefit, you need to assess each area independently.

Each section will include an overview and then an exercise to give you an insight into your priorities and goals for that area of your life. Each exercise should be listed by topic on a separate page in your journal. Take your time as this reflection and candid assessment is critical to the later steps for the process of designing your intentional life.

The Six Areas of Life

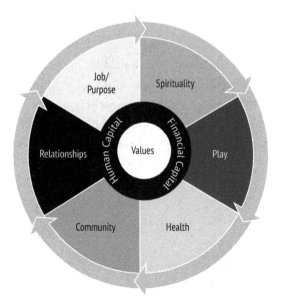

When we look at our money code, we need to look at what our past experience taught us in order to better understand how we got to where we are today. What are the memories, stories, activities that build our values, opinions, hopes, dreams, worries, and fears? This section will walk you through a list of exercises to build that historical perspective.

Relationships

Family, Friends, Communities

What are your earliest memories of family time? How did you spend time together? Did you play games, do puzzles, do outdoor activities?

Did your family travel to areas near or far? What are those places, and what are your memories?

| | |

For me, my family had a significant commitment to family vacations. We had the opportunity to explore new areas and cultures, try new activities, and spend quality time together. We visited national parks, learned how to ski locally, and then spent time at more remote skiing locations. These created great memories for me as a child.

When I was nine, my father was creating a significant new business in England and central Europe. As such, my parents planned for us to spend a summer overseas so that we could be with my father while also having the educational trip of a lifetime. During this trip, we also spent time with our relatives in England, developing relationships that are important to me, my husband, and children today. I am so thankful for that trip and how it influenced my curiosity for learning about other cultures and learning more about my family history.

| | |

How did your family spend the holidays?

How did your family value relationships? Did family members have honest conversations and/or were they more focused on activities?

Did you have unpaid duties or commitments that were part of your role and responsibility as a family member?

Who were you closest to and why?

Were there any negative surprises in relationships at a young age? This could include divorce or death, but also things that might be less serious yet still shocking to a young child. For example, a neighbor robbed our house, which was not as severe a shock as some other examples might be, but rattled my perception of trusting relationships with neighbors.

Job/Purpose

Career, Areas of Interest, Focus, Study, Where We Feel Valued and Validated

Did you have a job as a child? Summer job?

Did you do chores to earn your allowance or extra jobs to earn money?

Who were your job role models? Were there women and men role models? If so, what did they represent?

Sometimes storytelling helps get the juices flowing in your own thinking. My history includes my father sharing everything with me about his work, which in hindsight, was a gift. He shared his wins but also his failures and the lessons learned. In addition, he pushed me to work at a young age, which involved a newspaper route. I also sold light bulbs for a contest at school. These experiences taught me that I did like competition and seeing the results of hard work.

| | |

My father always pushed me to have a summer job. He wanted me to learn more about my strengths and weaknesses and potential areas of interest and passion. I learned quite a bit about what I might want or, conversely, would not want to do in the future.

The first time I saw a woman in a job different from nurse or teacher was when a cousin, who was a flight attendant, came to visit. I was seven years old and was fascinated by her. She shared how she loved traveling the world and showed real pride in her work. Reflecting on her visit, she was the first woman that I could really question about her job. The fact that there were many possible professions that I did not know about and would be open to women in the future was mind-blowing. I was also intrigued by her financial independence and flexibility to make different choices.

| | |

My father was the ultimate great job coach. He knew what he thought I should do but never told me. Instead, he asked a lot of good questions about the jobs that I had that I enjoyed. Some of these questions included: Were the jobs activity-based or research-based? Did they involve working alone, or did they include groups and interaction with others? His coaching allowed me to come to my own conclusions and, as a result, feel more conviction in the process.

My father was always pushing my boundaries and expectations. He also taught me that if you know that "no" is the worst answer, you should not fear saying it. Often it might even be expected. However, if you do not ask or do not reach for the "yes," you will never get it. What a gift he gave me!

Spirituality

Religion or a Sense of Higher Power, Centering Source, Mindfulness, Meditating, Praying

Did you go to a church, temple, mosque, or a religious institution?

Did you study religion or just attend?

Who were your role models for religious practice, and why?

Did you journal or take time to reflect as your younger self?

Did you journal or note experiences as a child, such as keeping a travel journal?

As a young girl, I was expected to go to Sunday School at the Presbyterian Church and to go through the confirmation process. I was never very interested in my own or other religions until I went to college and took religious courses. When it was better connected to culture and history, I became much more interested. I now see that I liked connecting the history of behavior and actions to religion in order to gain a better understanding. Also, my father had an interest in Buddhism. I cannot say that he adhered to any disciplined practice, but he liked the spirituality of the faith and how it was interwoven with both lifestyle and culture. I think that concept carried more connection for me. Today, spirituality, for me, is about the connection to my inner thoughts, nature, and those that I hold dear.

Play

Adaptability, Creativity, Exploration

What did you like to play as a child? In early childhood, middle school, high school?

What did you most enjoy about each of the above?

How did these activities make you feel, and why?

What lessons, behaviors, and values did they teach you?

What did you do to play together as a family? Did you attend sports, spectate, participate, or all of these?

The first time that I did this exercise, it was such an *aha* moment for me. As a young child, I loved to play kick-the-can. For those unfamiliar with the game, it is like hide-and-go-seek, only it adds in the element of a can. First, you hide. Once you are found or captured, you are put in jail. Only people who have not been captured can free you by sneaking in without the person who is "it" seeing them, and they kick the can to free everyone from jail. I loved finding clever hiding spots. Most of all, I loved "freeing" people. When I reflected on this, it is a direct connection to my passion today of freeing people from financial stress and other limitations so that they can enjoy their best life.

The second lesson from my reflection was that I liked playing aggressive team sports that required physical strength. Specifically, my two favorite team sports were soccer and hockey. I liked the feeling of being physically strong and playing games that, at the time, were considered a boy's sport. Perhaps, most of all, I loved playing a team sport where I not only learned to work on my individual skills, but also learned how I could be the best contributor to the success of the team. Those lessons are with me today as a leader.

Health

Activities, Role Modeling, Diet, Meals, Physical and Mental Strength

What were the rules in your childhood household around health, exercise, and food?

What were the healthy activities that your family did together?

Did anyone play organized sports? What was the commitment of the family to supporting players?

What sensations or emotions did you have around activity?

What emotions did you have around meals? Did your family eat together? Were meals healthy and balanced?

Did you have any issues around eating, such as anorexia, bulimia, compulsive eating, or binging? If so, what do you feel caused those behaviors? How did your family respond?

What messages did you receive in all the areas listed. above?

| | |

In our family, it was expected that we would be active. We were restricted to two hours of TV a week; therefore, we played outside most of the time. I learned to play football, street hockey, baseball, and tennis. I also learned how to swim, skate, hike, canoe, fish, and ride a minibike. We also spent a lot of time with our neighbors being active. Truthfully, I loved being outside with my brothers and learning their sports. The message I received from my father and brothers was that even as a girl it was OK to play traditional "boys" sports, especially when they were short players! The neighborhood was a tight-knit community that actively played together, and all ages were involved.

My parents were dedicated to our learning, being active and playing sports, and always being at practice. My mother made the big sacrifice of taking me to, not only after-school skating, but also before-school skating. Since she was not a morning person, this was hard for her, but I did feel supported. As siblings, we always went to one another's games and events. It was expected.

| | |

We ate together as a family almost every night. My mom cooked and waited for my father to get home; he was often late due to his demanding career. We did not always appreciate this, especially when we were very hungry and cranky kids. The only negative message was the "clean your plate" expectation, which led me to a habit of eating when I was not hungry anymore! I wish that we hadn't learned to always eat everything on our plates even if we were full. That being said, family dinners were also a wonderful time of connection and storytelling. My father could command an audience like no one else. He embellished stories and thrived on his captive audience.

Community

Giving Back Time, Money, Gifts, and Talents to Special Interest Groups Where You Volunteer

What were the expectations around volunteering or giving back to your community?

Who were your role models, and what did they do?

Were there nonfamily members who influenced you?

What did/have you done in terms of volunteering your time?

Did your family gift money to charitable organizations? If so, was there a focus or passion?

My mother volunteered quite a bit for the arts and particularly theatre organizations. She loved theatre and had wonderful experiences when she was part of the productions. My mom wanted to bring that opportunity to others. She knew how transformational a theatre experience could be, as it gets you to think differently. Perhaps it was really just experiencing the joy of good acting, a good story, or a wonderful musical. For my mom, the volunteer work, and helping others gave more meaning to her life, and that was a good lesson for us to see.

| | |

My father's role modeling was very different. He had a passion for helping those who had been incarcerated or had made bad choices. He felt that if given the right opportunity, these people could turn their lives around. He was all about giving second chances as everyone has made bad choices at some point in their life. My dad worked with judges to place those coming out of jail into jobs where they had the opportunity to work hard and make a better life for themselves. He also started a camp for youth to help give them the discipline and hard work ethic to get back on track. A memorable and powerful lesson came the night when my father received a lifetime achievement award for his accomplishments. Instead of focusing on his success, he used the spotlight to share the mistakes he made, and the lessons he learned to help others make better decisions and do better work. While he did express his gratitude in his speech, he also taught us all that if you have the spotlight, use it for doing good and helping others rather than focusing on yourself.

Now look back at this section. What were the rules in your home when you were growing up, and how did they relate to the six areas? You can be specific or just answer them in a generalized manner. Which rules have you adopted? Did you decide then or in the future to do the opposite of what you were taught or learned by their behavior? What are you taking forward for you and/or your partner/ spouse and/or kids?

"Because once we feel, know, and dare to imagine more for ourselves, we cannot unfeel, unknow, or unimagine. There is no going back."

—Glennon Doyle

CHAPTER ELEVEN

TODAY: UNDERSTANDING THE INTERCONNECTION OF EACH AREA

Relationships

Family, Friends, Communities

Build a diagram that starts with you in the middle. Then draw a line for each type or category of relationships in your life. Each branch of this tree or diagram should represent relationships in different aspects of your life: family, work, communities, school friends, relationships through sports, interest groups, or kids' activities.

For family, build additional lines/branches off any family member that leads to a new "branch" of the family. For example, if you have a spouse or partner, add a branch from them to their direct relatives (your in-laws). If you have a close extended family, you might want to include cousins, etc.

I I I

Now go through and circle in BLUE those who are the most important relationships in your life. Then, circle in GREEN those relationships that are the most positive; you can have more than one color on any person. Lastly, circle the most negative or toxic relationships in RED. YELLOW should identify those relationships to which you wish to devote more time and energy. Again, any name can have more than one color. This exercise is for you, so be honest!

Job/Purpose

Career, Areas of Interest, Focus, Study, Where We Feel Valued and Validated

In this assessment, you will need to start with a new sheet of paper. The purpose is to show where you spend your time and what brings you joy, or conversely, what drains you. Most important, if you undervalue your job or roles, you likely also undervalue your self-worth. Sometimes this can be caused by not spending time really looking at all your interests, whether they be career-focused or other pursuits.

On your sheet, begin to free-form answers to the following questions.

- What is the meaning of your work for others? For you?

| | |

Use as much description as you need but with a message that resonates with a punch!

- What are the messages that you have received over the years about your work or time spent on interests that stand out to you?

Some examples from my stories show that there is a women's pay gap and discrimination, which shows that women are not treated as equal to men. Overt discrimination in my own career has led me to create and embrace scorecards, transparency and accountability. Contribution and performance can always be measured, often quantitatively but also qualitatively. Demonstrated positive treatment of others and behaviors as well as values can be as measurable as quantitative success metrics.

How people communicated in life and business can be as or more important than what they communicate. I was in a meeting several years ago in which a coworker described a man's strength by saying he had balls. When he realized I was in the room, the man further belittled me by saying he didn't know what term to use that applied to women. I responded that it didn't matter because we used our brains! Here I experienced the condescending reference to women but also felt proud of my good comeback line! This section should highlight messages that you received that you have never forgotten because they created some sort of emotional reaction.

- Be sure to include in this section a record of everything that demands your time, whether it is a responsibility or a need.

| | |

For example, if you wear multiple hats in a job, list those different aspects separately. If you are involved in eldercare or childcare for your family, list those things too. Now, go through each one of these items and put a colored dot next to them or circle them following these guidelines:

- BLUE is what is most important to or required of you.
- GREEN is what brings you joy, positive feeling, a sense of being valued.
- RED is what drains you, creates negative feelings or energy.
- YELLOW for what you wish you could do more of or explore more.

Again, each item can have one or more colors.

Spirituality

Religion or a Sense of Higher Power and Centering Source, Mindfulness, Meditating, Praying

Exploring what you do for your personal spirituality, write out what you have and/or currently do in terms of religious experiences. This should include any activities that you do either within a religious building but also at home or in nature.

- Do you say a blessing before eating, and what are the characteristics of that activity? Then list out anything that you do to reflect or meditate.
- Do you have or did you ever have a gratitude journal or practice?

- Do you use an hour in the church to reflect? Do you meditate, and if so, how often and for how long?

| | |

Be sure to include other mindful exercises that you do and write them down. Clarity breaks or similar practices, such as delegate/elevate activities, would be appropriate to list here. Now go through your list and identify, using the following colors:

- BLUE are those that are most important because of a family commitment to church/temple etc.
- GREEN are those that you find most valuable.
- RED is used to identify those that have a negative impact on you.
- YELLOW is for those items that you would like to expand upon or do more of.

Play

Adaptability, Creativity, Exploration

What do you do on weekends, vacations, and during your free time?
Make a list of the things that you do for *you*!
Do you read, travel, garden, play sports, plan time/trips with special friends?

Now go through each of these and color-code them:

- BLUE is to note what is important or required.
- GREEN is what brings you the most joy.

- RED is for what drains you (for example, mandatory trips with the family that are not to your favorite places).
- YELLOW is for what you want to do more of in life.

I I I

Does anything jump out as an *aha* moment or wake-up call for you?

Health

Activity, Role Modeling, Diet, Meals, Strength, Physical, and Mental

What activities do you do for your physical health?

What good and bad habits do you have, or what do you practice around diet? Be sure to include both the good and the bad and be honest!

I battled anorexia in college, and it is important to look at things like this and understand what caused it. Vulnerability, reflection, and awareness are critical in this exercise. For me, there was that phase of my life and its impact on my mental and physical health. In time I have realized that my experience impacted my family and children as well.

Do you take supplements?

Do you keep regular doctor appointments?

Do you do anything specific for brain development?

Do you drink alcohol, have dessert or sweets, are you vegan or vegetarian, or have other eating habits that may positively or negatively affect your health?

| | |

Do you have special workout plans or classes that you take?

Please list out all these things and color code in:

- BLUE is what is critical or important.
- GREEN is what bring you joy, a good feeling.
- RED is what you do not like or has a negative feeling for you (colonoscopy and/or mammogram would go here for most of us!).
- YELLOW is for what you would like to do more of or is on your wish list.

Community

Giving Back Time, Money, or Your Gifts/Talents, Special Interest Groups Where You Volunteer

List out all the volunteer or charitable organizations that you are involved with or where you contribute your time. In some cases, you might have had a long-term connection that you are no longer active with (volunteering your time or resources) but want to list because you still feel connected to them.

| | |

Look at your checkbook or tax return and list where you have given money or other gifts of monetary value (stock gifts, property etc.). Do these gifts and the total amounts by organization or area of focus reflect your priorities and values?

- BLUE is what is critical or important.
- GREEN is what brings you joy, a good feeling.
- RED is what you do not like or that has a negative feeling for you.
- YELLOW is for what you would like to do more of or is on your wish list.

"Comparing yourself to others is an act of violence against your authentic self."

—Iyanla Vanzant

CHAPTER TWELVE

HUMAN CAPITAL AND FINANCIAL CAPITAL = THE HOW

Earlier, we explored the Fear Zone, which is the period of avoidance and anxiety that immobilizes us. This can become a circular behavior because avoidance feeds anxiety, and anxiety breeds avoidance. When we are in this phase, we need to look at what actions get us closer to or farther away from what we want. How can we break out of our perceived limitations, which are often self-imposed?

A good analogy here is to think about a time when we were physically injured. For me, I herniated two discs in my back, ironically, working out with a trainer. The pain was extreme, and after multiple injections, I had to endure a period of inactivity and rest. Anyone that knows me could verify that I am not very good at either of those things! My plan for recovery was an exercise plan to build strength gradually with each step building on the previous step. That is understandable. But I was in excellent shape before the injury, so when the generic protocol was applied to me, I was kicked out of physical therapy after four sessions. I was at the average strength that they hoped to achieve with most patients. However, I am a hockey player, skier, and generally a very active person who loves working out. After my injury, I lived in the Fear Zone. What if I did too much and ended up reinjuring myself? I was not sure I could go through that kind of pain again. What if I went to another trainer who pushed me too hard? Perhaps the scariest for me was the worry that I would be hurt so much that I could not play the sports that I loved. What if I was forever restricted from physical activity?

| | |

My anxiety had paralyzed me. I decided to research and find a physical therapist who was used to working with athletes. That was step one, and I found her relatively quickly. Her process and expectations were higher, and her methods tailored better to someone like me. This put me into my Learning Zone, where I now had a clear plan of the next steps. She was getting me ready to move to the Confidence Zone where my body would be better prepared for the expected demands but also more resilient to withstand strenuous activities on my back as I aged this would be the equivalent of a plan for the expected and unexpected life transitions. While I can't say that I will never get a back injury again, I know that if I stay disciplined by doing the strength training, stretching, and other preventative steps, I will be able to do more of what I love for a longer period.

In this case, I was aligning my human capital, time, and financial resources to help me accomplish a primary goal of being able to be active again without fear of hurting myself. It was gradual, incremental, and cost perhaps more than I wanted to pay; however, I was back playing hockey, hiking, working out, and skiing within a year. Without developing the plan that got me away from my fear and anxiety, I would never be able to get back to the life I wanted.

| | |

Are some things different today in terms of what I know to do and not do? Absolutely! But I had hired a great coach to get me there and teach me the best path to move forward. A good coach and a customized plan can pull you out of fear and anxiety to see a future more consistent with what you need. A good coach understands how to connect your "why" or values and priorities to your "what," which is the important activities in the six areas of life: relationships, job/purpose, spirituality, play, health, and community.

"How" is our human capital defined as time, personal contribution (nonmonetary), physical presence, intellectual insight, etc. This is our most precious asset and needs to be managed well. "How" is also our financial capital or the monetary contribution that is required to achieve our "what."

| | |

If we know that our human capital and financial capital are limited, then we must prioritize to ensure we choose to apply it in the most meaningful ways for ourselves and our family. Meaningful is fine; however, we need to know what reduces stress, gives you joy, and gives meaning to your lives. Here is the best way to start that process.

Go through the six areas and pick one or two things in each that you would like to focus on first. Then estimate the cost, in terms of human capital (time and intellectual effort), and financial cost/outlay. How does financial capital facilitate, enable, limit, or prohibit you from achieving this? It is helpful to chart this out.

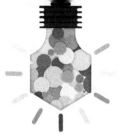

"You can't be that kid standing at the top of the waterslide, overthinking it. You have to go down the chute."

—Tina Fey

CHAPTER THIRTEEN

DEVELOPING PSYCHOLOGICAL FLEXIBILITY

This next step is about helping you understand that YOU HAVE CHOICES! Perhaps the following framework will give you tools to help make those choices and decisions.

There is a framework used by some therapists entitled ACT, which stands for Acceptance and Commitment Therapy. It breaks down our behaviors into two areas: first, there are your valued guided actions, and second, there are those mindful actions that you take.

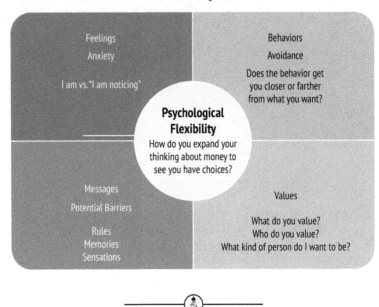

ACT = Acceptance + Commitment Therapy

1) Values-guided action
2) Mindful action

Create a rich and meaningful life while acception that pain, loss, frustration, disappointment, and failure come along with it.

Feelings
Anxiety

I am vs. "I am noticing"

Behaviors
Avoidance

Does the behavior get you closer or farther from what you want?

Psychological Flexibility
How do you expand your thinking about money to see you have choices?

Messages
Potential Barriers
Rules
Memories
Sensations

Values

What do you value?
Who do you value?
What kind of person do I want to be?

Here we will explore how to look at our feelings and behaviors almost as if we were an outsider looking in on them rather than being wrapped up in them at the moment. As you look at these different choices, ask yourself what feelings does each one evokes. As you answer the questions, use the response of "I am noticing" versus "I am ..."

| | |

Why do we do this? It is simply because "I am" statements often create negative feelings and anxiety. By looking at each feeling from the outside, it permits you to mindfully reframe the action as a behavior and not defining who you are as a person. Part of this reflection should also include how you see this behavior as related to messages, rules, memories, or sensations, as opposed to your defining you.

Let me give an example that will perhaps be helpful. As I mentioned earlier, when I was in college, I battled anorexia. For those who had a similar challenge controlling their eating or lack of eating, the disorder stems most often from a desire to feel like you are in control. At the root of my insecurity was a feeling that I was letting other people down. I had image and acceptance issues about my body and had gone from feeling like a big person on campus in high school to feeling less well known and understood in college. So, the control over my eating, dropping weight, and getting skinny felt good. Unfortunately, I got to a dangerous state of no periods, no body fat, and altogether lack of nutrition.

| | |

The messages I was sending out were "I am not pretty," "I am fat," "I am not as smart as most everyone here," "I am not living up to expectations," etc. I blamed others, including my parents, for how I felt. I snowballed the whole situation by taking anything anyone said and piling it onto myself with statements like "see, they are disappointed in me. I am a loser." I was in a fixed mindset of blame. I even took gestures of love, like my brother Tom driving seven hours to see me and try to help me, as him not trusting me. I was creating my own pain and suffering.

As my sophomore ice hockey season started, I was getting pushed around because I did not have the weight or the strength to hold my own. After getting Rookie of The Year in my freshman year, I was playing poorly, and throwing away my good habits while feeling sorry for myself. I was losing something which brought me joy and connected me with teammates and coaches whom I adored. I am not exactly sure when and where I totally put it all together, but I awakened to the fact that, in this case, I was the one creating my own problems. I chose to get my act together. I began eating again and gained strength as I put on muscle weight. I noticed that if I took better care of myself, I felt better, and I played better.

| | |

I decided that I wanted to be the best player and, most especially, the best teammate that I could be. Because I was not and will never be a player with a lot of talent, I chose to work as hard or harder than everyone else. My passion and focus were around being the teammate that I wanted to be and helping our team win in any way that I could. I would never be a high scorer or the fastest. But I could be a role player for our team. I "shadowed" or chased down the best player on the opposing team. With my strong skating, from years of being a figure skater, I could chase down and annoy the best opponents. I had been given this amazing college opportunity to play sports at the highest level, and I needed to rededicate myself to my team and improve my health and ability and skills to serve that team. By junior year I had won Unsung Hero and was named Co-Captain for my senior year. I was lucky that I had a second chance to get my act together and do more for my team.

The lessons here are that I started defining myself by what I was feeling. Instead of using statements like "I am noticing that I don't feel as confident in myself due to some new challenges," I embraced "I am a loser," or "I am letting other people down." No one ever said such a thing; it was all me that was making it my reality through my anorexia.

| | |

It took time for me to start understanding that it was my choice not to eat and that I was the one who allowed my health and my hockey career tank. It was also my choice to turn it around and reframe it in a more positive way. I needed to celebrate all the choices that would lead to better outcomes. I better defined what role I could play successfully and feel good about in terms of my contribution. I created smaller goals, steps, and milestones to help me reach the big goal of playing at least at the level before my downslide and hopefully better. Good choices each and every day led to better results. These included better health, better play, better contribution to my team, and, perhaps most important, better self-esteem.

By no means was it all forward movement. I had my days where I made bad decisions on eating, training, or allowing negative messages to get me down. But with the sunrise always came a new day to develop new and better habits. To be certain, repeating good behaviors, building a better mindset, and awareness would be my next best steps to recovery and reaching my goals.

Building Your Own Portfolio of Goals

Perhaps the biggest lesson to note, as we determine what choices we have and what path we want to pick, is that it is our personal journey. What everyone else thinks is not nearly as relevant as what those who understand our values and priorities think. When we are honest with ourselves, what really matters? This is a vulnerability that can be frightening and paralyzing. It takes courage to show up when you are trying something new, changing course, and cannot necessarily control the outcome. But our comfort can be built around asking more questions such as:

- Where does my energy come from? What generates energy for me?
- What really excites me or motivates me?
- What is in it for me? (It is OK to ask this question, especially when you are asking it in reference to your values.)

| | |

Now go through your list and pick three to five items that you want to focus on and revamp. Also, ask the following questions:

- What is your next step for each?
- Who or what can help you take that next step?

For example, I need to meet with my boss to get a better understanding of my career path. I might also engage a career coach. Often, I find a mentor or sponsor can provide some context for how I might think about and frame that dialogue to be constructive and productive for both of us.

Another example is when I want to get in better shape. The next step is often researching what activities or group classes that I could attend with a friend or coworker or meeting a personal trainer who can keep me motivated and committed. During COVID quarantine, for example, I started a virtual session twice a week with two coworkers in which we work on strength training, flexibility, and balance. Just having that time set aside with each other ensures that we are committing to getting in better shape!

| | |

Now pick three to five things you can stop doing! You have not won the lottery with there now being 26 hours in your day, so you will have to cut out some weaker or less healthy behaviors to make room for the new and improved choices and actions! Saying no should be viewed as saying yes to something more substantial.

In the economy and market declines of 2008–2009, I knew that my kids were concerned because my job was tied to the economy and markets. They were hearing a lot about parents losing jobs.

| | |

Jeff and I could have avoided the subject and let everyone in the family become more anxious since we had two big challenges that we had to address in a healthy way. One was that our income would be lower, and we had to reduce expenses.

Second, we had a teachable moment and could really delve into where we were spending our money and see if it was consistent with our values. This analysis would be healthier than just watching our bank account values dwindle while we stayed denial and fear of taking things away.

|||

The whole process was much easier than we ever thought it could be in actuality. Jeff and I went through all the expenses. We also used the lens of our core family values of spending quality time together, education, and good health to determine what would stay and what would go. We realized in our analysis that we were spending a lot of money eating out, which was both expensive and less healthy. We moved to more meal preparation for the week, which causes less waste and is more cost-effective. Jeff and I knew that we wanted to pay for our kid's education and would cut back almost everything else to provide that for them.

Finally, we wanted to have vacations still, but we could drive rather than fly, saving both airfare and rental car expenses, as well as rent less expensive accommodations.

|||

Most important, we called a family meeting to go over our choices with our kids. When one balked at us cutting out cable tv, I told her she could pay for it if she wanted to keep it. She reflected and said we really do not watch it anymore, and it is a luxury that we do not need. Our family all learned a lot through that process, and we felt good because our decisions were consistent with our values. We gave up things that were not as important as others and sometimes decided to look at things with a new and less costly approach. There were trade-offs to be sure. Informed choices that were aligned with our values won out over spending on items we wanted but were not essential.

As you go through this step of building your portfolio of goals, it is important to choose your support team. These are the people around you who can help with the hard stuff and hold you accountable to your values and positive steps. I have noticed over the past decade that the most successful people in life are the ones who surround themselves with truly good friends and partners. I define a true friend or partner as someone who is a cheerleader. They are also the first person to challenge you when you are doing something inconsistent with a stated value or priority. True friends are your reality check. My best friend, Pat, does not let me get away with anything that is not true to the person I am and want to be, and I love her for it!

Building accountability into your journey is very important. There are a few strategies that might be helpful. First, saying something out loud to an accountability partner and asking for check-ins can be very effective. Utilize this person at least once a month, if not more frequently. You can teleconference or be in person. But you both need to devote the time for you to get their insights through good questions and thoughtful feedback.

When I let my calendar start running me rather than me controlling with whom I meet and when I ask for help. I got an accountability partner that was outside of my business and my inner circle of friends, but I knew they would be very honest. We would talk for half an hour every other week about strategies and whether I was adhering to them, what the results were, and any new developments. She asked me to wait 24–48 hours before saying yes to commitments. During that time, I was to really think if the new commitment was consistent with my priorities and goals. She emphasized that every time I said "yes" to something, I was saying "no" to something else. I would not always know what it was that I was saying no to at the decision-making time. She also asked that on each Friday, I sit down and look for appointments that could come off my calendar for the following week! These are the first two steps that I took, and having an accountability partner to whom I had to report ensured that I stayed true to my commitments and myself.

| | |

There are people who choose to be victims and blame others for everything that goes wrong and do not take ownership. Interestingly they often have shifting groups of friends: no one sticks around because their friendships are relatively superficial. They are the first to blame and avoid problem solving because, of course, it is not them who could be the source or cause of the issue. My husband, Jeff, used to say when our kids were little, "If you don't like how they are acting, hold up the mirror!" People who blame others typically are not good at owning their own behavior and consequences of their choices. They are often complacent and self-absorbed. A good alternative is to reframe the situation. If you do not like how people treat you, then hold up the mirror and ask:

- Am I a good coworker, friend, and family member?
- Am I trying to solve issues and problems rather than just complaining?
- What specifically can I do to engage others and improve the situation?
- Am I trying to reduce the stress of others by being clear, helpful, and taking ownership?

- Do I recognize the valued contribution of others and the potential benefits to many?

If you do the work on values and choices, I will bet you can answer most of these questions with a resounding "Yes!" If you cannot, you might want to reread this chapter and do the hard work on your values and choices!

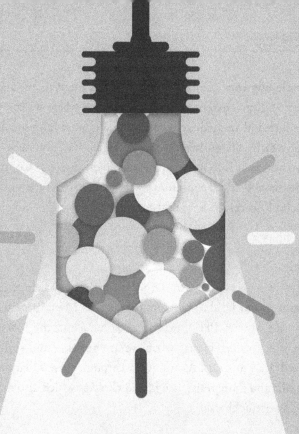

PART V

BUILDING YOUR LUMINATION PLAN

"You can be the lead in your own life."

—Kerry Washington

Developing your plan takes courage, resiliency, focus, and honesty. Unfortunately, it is not an elevator where we can punch the number and immediately go there. We must take small steps, some of which will work and some of which will not work. Along the way, you will face uncertainty and likely anxiety. Contrary to what media and society often message to us, anxiety is not bad if it is in check. It can be a catalyst for positive reflection and change.

Anxiety is what gets us to reframe or find someone to help us reframe a dialogue in our head to be more productive. My favorite psychologist, Lisa Damour, PHD, explained to me about the Inoculation Theory. The concept is that when we are growing and shifting in life, it will lead to stress. As you work through these situations, you build skills and more resistance to bad choices, which also may lead to making better choices.

| | |

We are on a journey, and we need to build our core strengths and tenets for positivity and growth as well as accept our limits and boundaries to get us there—training our minds the same way we train our bodies. We build core strength to help keep our bodies safe from injury. In our minds, we need to build that same core strength and focus on our own needs and priorities. While we will have stress from unexpected challenges and life transitions, sometimes we are running so fast we do not hear the message or see the meaning right in front of us. We try to keep up with everyone else; be the best in someone else's definition rather than being the best for ourselves and family.

My favorite example comes from my daughter Emily when she was five years old and in kindergarten. As a working mom, I felt guilty that I did not have time to research and sign her up for all the best after-school activities. When I read off a list of possibilities, she asked, "Mom, this is my first time going to school all day. Can I just get through that and see what I want to do later? Do I really have to decide now?" Out of the mouths of babes! This was such a good perspective from a five-year-old, compared to the rushed decision-making of her mom of 37 years, at the time.

Your journey is yours to own. In previous chapters, we covered reflection of your personal history, exercises to raise awareness of your values journey and priorities, how to build a process and a plan, and tools to maintain fortitude, strength, and focus on your core values and beliefs. Now we will explore how you stay the course through planned and unplanned life transitions and challenges.

*"Step out of the history that is holding you back.
Step into the new story you are willing to create."*

—Oprah Winfrey

CHAPTER FOURTEEN

TRIGGERS, BARRIERS, AND SPEED BUMPS = LIFE HAPPENS

If we use the physical metaphor of financial fitness or financial strength, we also can begin to understand why we hit snags in our own progress and tempo of our lives when we get hurt. Physical injury typically happens because something is not in balance or is causing stress. We have overused a particular muscle or area of our body without developing enough protection to prevent hurting ourselves. As I mentioned earlier, a few years ago, I incurred a back injury. I wanted to blame the trainer who pushed me when I was already sore and feeling below par. However, the truth is that I was not direct in my vulnerability and openness about the fact that I felt weak that day and needed to avoid being physically active. Instead of listening to my body, I defaulted to my drive to workout, get stronger, and do more.

Once injured, we then must put together a slow step by step recovery program, in order to rebuild and refocus. Whether we like it or not, there is an age appropriateness to our recovery plan. Sadly, as we age, recovery takes longer! As is true with all injuries, but especially with a back injury, we must focus on our core strength. Everything emanates from core strength, which helps prevent injury and allows us to pivot, flex, have good balance, and power drive to other parts of our bodies.

| | |

The real world is much the same. We must go back to Chapter Nine and remind ourselves to build our physical and mental resiliency. This is imperative so that we can rebuild our bodies and our minds, to perform better out of habit. This is the overall point of fitness and strength.

In life, our core helps us build grit or strength of character. When we lose our core, our focus becoming unbalanced, leading to the potential to be hurt and in pain. In family situations, I have a history of trying to make everyone happy, which more often ends up with disappointment in myself. It often leads to me owning another person's behavior rather than focusing on my own.

| | |

When I was in my early 30s, one of my brothers was in constant friction with our dad. I kept trying to fix their relationship and became the go-between. Rather than helping them to communicate directly, I was pulled into being a messenger, because it was easier for my brother to talk to me than for him to talk to our dad. I was miserable and frustrated, and my relationship with both of them was negatively impacted.

A wise psychologist told me that I would never be able to fix the main problem and that I should appreciate that neither of them had an issue with me. Maintain your healthy relationships and give them more strength to develop by refusing to be caught in the middle.

My family does have a history of not hearing the word "no," which meant that changing my role took more than one attempt. When my brother brought his "dad" issues to me, I said that I would no longer be their go-between. I did not have a problem with dad or with him, for that matter. His problem was with dad, and therefore, the only way that it would get better is if he figured out how to talk to dad in a more constructive way. After the third push by my brother, he finally realized that I really meant no. Guess what? His relationship with Dad improved! Best of all, my relationship with both improved, as well.

| | |

Positivity and a growth mindset are critical to helping us build our core strength. Unfortunately, most of us spend our days thinking that we do not have enough or are not good enough or didn't get enough done. We see only the gaps. We do not spend enough time celebrating what is good, what we have accomplished, what went well that day, and what we are grateful for at the end of the day. We must spend more time on the GAIN.

Science shows that positive thoughts generate positive energy sources: There is an analysis called the The Gap and The Gain. Typically strong drivers and achievers are quick to move past the "gains" or accomplishments. They don't spend a lot of time celebrating successes. Rather they move to the evident gaps, what still needs to be fixed or addressed. This behavior can really zap the energy out of those around them as it feels as if more focus is always on what needs to improve rather than what has been accomplished.

Personally, I have worked with my coach to remember to celebrate personal success. I am quick to celebrate others, but lousy at acknowledging or spending much time celebrating my own achievements. Like many women, I don't like being in the limelight. Further I tend to dismiss the gains and continue to focus on my own gaps.

Remember, try to balance the time you focus on the Gap with the time you focus on the Gain. Earlier I wrote about my viewpoint that the most successful people that I know are those who surround themselves with strong, authentic people and friends who will speak the truth and challenge the person when needed and offer support when needed, as well. They will force you to stop and celebrate your gains and accomplishments. And when you have real challenges, having a team around you will help you to find the best resources and get you through the hard stuff. They will be your mirror and your champions.

| | |

True partners and friends recognize the positive and call you on the carpet when you are not true to yourself and your values. These are the same people who will help you find the resources to get through the hard stuff in life. They do not judge based on society but help you to see that the only judge that counts is you. You are the best person to know if your plans are consistent with your values and priorities.

When our kids were young, a common trigger for me was my internal guilty mom complex. What I learned was that asking for help and being able to afford help was a gift; this was not something that meant I was less than a good mom. We had Evie, our nanny, who became an important member of our family. She shared our values, our priorities, our approach to discipline and accountability, and our love of our children.

| | |

Evie also came from a very difficult background and upbringing and brought a helpful perspective and viewpoint to our lives. She taught our children about true hardship and discrimination. Evie's stories helped shape our children's tenets. It was good for them to understand compassion for others through her stories. Evie was a partner in raising our kids, not replacing us. She aligned with us on values and priorities and magnifying the time we had with our kids to ensure it would be our best time.

It was a choice that worked well for us, a choice that might be right for some and wrong for others. The gift was that she was the perfect fit for us. Our partnership in raising our children with her showed our kids that it is OK to need help and find a partner who shares your values and priorities. We were blessed to find someone who shared our values and priorities in raising our children. She was candid, supportive but firm, and gave us the wonderful gift of comfort that our kids were in good hands when we were at work. She treated our children as her own and gave us 19 years of her life. Many people don't believe in having additional care to help with children. For us, Evie was a benefit and a relationship that changed our kids' lives forever for the better. I will forever feel judged for this choice, but at the end of the day, the positive role that Evie had in our kid's lives and our lives was a precious gift.

| | |

At the other end of the spectrum, managing eldercare for my parents was and is the toughest job of my life and often a barrier to me having time to take care of myself. Rather than the days where you give your children time, attention, and resources, and watch them grow and thrive, you do the same with your parents and watch a slow decline. Is it better than it would be if you did not do all those things? Yes! But the challenges are even tougher, and the stress seems bigger because the solutions feel more complicated and incremental at best.

Eldercare is time-consuming and emotionally draining. The physical decline of elders makes it hard for their children to get them to do new activities to build their strength, as well as to address their problems and face reality. The only anecdote is surrounding yourself with people who are experts in this space or have gone through it themselves. They are the partners you need. We can wallow in being a victim or take the positive approach of finding the next best step. Researching our choices and asking others who have been through a similar journey for their assistance helps us to manage this journey. We must build the team, generate family dialogues, and find resources that help us move forward in the most constructive way possible.

| | |

About two years after my father died, I went to "Caring for the Caregiver" week at Canyon Ranch in Tucson as a gift from my mother. In a session, I was asked to list off all the people that I cared for daily. After naming several family members, my widowed mom, widowed clients, and some clients and friends going through divorce or trauma, I burst into tears. I realized that I had been so busy caregiving that I had never grieved for the loss of my father. I had not taken time to breathe from the oxygen mask as I was too busy putting it on everyone else. I was quickly digging myself into a hole of despair and sadness.

As caregivers, we can lose perspective quickly due to the continuous twists and turns of unexpected demands. We must get help and build in time to restore and renew our energy and mind. Society sometimes leads us to believe that we must do it all ourselves. This could not be farther from the truth. We must bring in others and additional resources so that when we are caregiving and helping those we love, we are able to be a source of strength and positive energy. If we are exhausted, we become frustrated and short-tempered. Then we feel guilty because we are not giving our best self to that person.

| | |

In my own journey, I am the primary caregiver and help my widowed mother. With my Superwoman complex, I originally felt I had to be there at every appointment and always on call. The truth is, I do not have the patience, let alone the time, to do it all while also pursuing a full-time career. In addition, every time a crisis hit, like when my mom ended in the hospital, I stopped taking care of myself.

I ate poorly, stopped working out, and was not getting enough sleep. The cycle was terrible for both of us. Because I was extended beyond my capacity, both physically and mentally, I was not able to be as supportive and open-minded as I needed to be for her.

Through research, I found and hired a senior care manager to help take my mom to appointments and coordinating parts of her health-care needs. This has been transformational in my relationship with my mother. No longer do I get frustrated and stressed trying to manage all the appointments and having a short fuse if she does not do what she is supposed to do for herself. Rather I have a partner who is a good advocate for my mom while being a new friend, as well, sharing some of her special interests like theatre and opera. Moreover, I have someone who is a great sounding board and thought partner. The best part is I can now spend more quality time with my mom on our shared interests and having more "fun" together. We are closer than we have ever been to one another. All of this is because I finally recognized my shortcomings, asked for help, and focused my time and energy on what brought mutual connection and joy to my mom and me.

| | |

When we can take time to reflect, restore, and renew, we can make informed decisions. As a result, we can be better for others, generating more positive energy and feelings for them, as well. Simply, if we live a long life, we will have many friends and family who will be in trauma, decline, pain, or sickness. To be a good caregiver, we must give ourselves permission to take the time and get help to be more effective for ourselves and those we love.

In this chapter, I reviewed some of my triggers and barriers and the solutions that helped me. We are all unique. What triggers get you off track? What are the potential solutions? Who can help you identify solutions and resources? Who are those friends who can help you speak your truth, and what is best for you in a crisis or challenging situation?

"Above all, be the heroine of your life, not the victim."

—Nora Ephron

CHAPTER FIFTEEN

STAGES OF DEVELOPMENT AND OUR RELATIONSHIP TO MONEY

Money is never just money! Earlier, we explored our money code, our history, and messages that have framed our relationship to money. Now we will look at today and our future. In this way, we may find money is part of our scarcity mindset; there is never enough, or we may lose it all. We are fearful of our future. Will we have a sufficient amount of money? Will we lose it, earn it, or be worthy of getting paid enough? Clearly, self-esteem and self-worth are often tied to our relationship with money.

Everyone has their own ideal as it relates to money. Do you want to make money because you see it as a measure of success or because you want enough or fear not having enough? With money comes responsibility. We cannot ignore it or forget it. In addition, the value of money changes over time. In our younger years and when it is scarcer, it is a direct need. We must have money to pay rent, buy food, etc. As we get older, we develop more of an indirect need. We have more choices around how we allocate our resources, including money. It is important to recognize that how we prioritize our spending is a way for us to change or enhance our experiences and relationships.

Stages and Key Influences During Different Stages of Development

The Early Years

	YOUNG CHILD	TEEN	YOUNG ADULT
RELATIONSHIP	• Trust • Parents/Family • Teachers • Independence	• Trust • Challenging barriers with safe foundation • Beginnings of Intimacy	• Developing Intimacy Isolation • Affirmation/Connection
COMMUNITY	• Family • Friend Groups • Developing Values/Resilience	• Friend Groups • Family • Other affiliations via interests	• Environment • Social Concerns • Expression
JOB/PURPOSE	• Learner • Develop Independence	• Student • Athlete • Performer • Learner	• Early Career • Exploration/Self-Learning • Striving
SPIRITUAL	• Fear > Affirmation	• Religion • Yoga or meditation	• Religion/Meditation • Sense of Higher Power
HEALTH	• Hunger • Muscle Development • Strength • Sleep	• Mental Health • Athleticism • Body Image	• Exercise • Nutrition
PLAY	• Intellectual Games • Imitation • Creative/Unstructured	• Social Identity	• Travel/Exploration • Defining Interests
TRIGGERS/BARRIERS/ OPPORTUNITIES	• Injury • Lack of Trust of Key People • Trauma • Learning Differences	• Social pressures • Anxiety/stress • Social Media	• Job Change/Career Path • Pay/Debt/Credit • Limited Resources • Poor Choices • Having Children

Mid-Life Years through Later Stages

	MID-LIFE YEARS	ENCORE YEARS	LATE STAGES
RELATIONSHIP	• Family Redefined • Responsibility • Commitment	• Generational • Contribution • Validation • meaning	• Compassion • Acceptance • Consciousness & Choices • Dependence

COMMUNITY	• Connection to like-
	  minded/Situation
	• Community Importance
		• Charitable
		• Give Back
		• Pay It Forward
			• Shrinking
			• Staying engaged intellectually
			  and physically

JOB/PURPOSE	• Job becomes purpose for pay • Sense of efficacy/Professionalism	• Meaningful • Contribution • Non-Judgmental	• Sharing family values and history • Wisdom/Knowledge
SPIRITUAL	• Stress Management/Therapy	• Forgiveness • Imperfection • Love of Self • Others	• Forgiveness • Connection
HEALTH	• Commitment • Supplements • Brain & Physical Health	• Adaptation • Acceptance • Prevention • Brain health	• Mental health • Prevention • Care Partners • Cognitive Decline
PLAY	• Travel • Group Trips–Girls/College Friends • Defining Interests	• Generational • "Experiences" • Value of Relationships with other women	• Social interaction • Family
TRIGGERS/ BARRIERS/ OPPORTUNITIES	• Relationship Triangle • Own Parent Health • Job Loss/Change • Financial Misuse • Children Challenges	• Sufficient Funds • Access to Healthcare • Injury • Loss of spouse/partner/friends • Exercise of mind/body	• Lack of Exercise/Stimuli • Elder Abuse • Sufficient Funds • Independence or Loss • Dependence on others • Loneliness/Isolation

This development chart was created to look at the ages and stages of development and the intersection of the six different areas of our lives. Each of these areas ultimately also connects with three resources: time, money, and self-worth. Money is defined as our human capital and our financial capital. Both have value and are in demand at each stage. We must recognize that our lives are an evolution through stages, priorities, and choices, some of which we control, and some of which feel as if they control us. Through this chart, perhaps we can see that we are more similar than we are different and can find guidance from coaches, counselors, advisors, and others who have lived through a similar situation.

It is critical to understand that at every stage, we are testing our defined meaning for money, time, and self-worth. It is never static and is not random in its transition. We are continually changing our priorities. We shift the areas of importance in our lives based on current circumstances. To understand this, think back 10 or perhaps 20 years and make a list of what was important to you at that time in the six areas. It is likely very different from what you feel is important today. Now reflect on how you felt about yourself during that time. How did you spend your financial and human capital? How did you allocate your time to meet the demands of your life?

| | |

As we go through these stages, we do not always know what might trip us up, especially as we get older. We often have more relationships and demands, which leads to more influences that can impact our lives. It is telling that as we age and grow, we see our parents as more human and change our expectations of them. We have a temporal perspective, along with our developmental perspective.

As you find your stage on this chart, what area or areas feel like they are in the best sync or rhythm? What areas feel as though you need to explore more closely, as they are creating anxiety and fear?

| | |

As we outlined in the Lumination Comfort Zone progression, you need to take one step and learn more in those areas. What is the next best step to take to learn more about your source of stress or anxiety and how you might move forward? What information do you need? What could help to get you closer to the Confidence Zone and away from the Fear or Learning Zone?

*"The most difficult thing is the decision to act;
the rest is merely tenacity."*

—Amelia Earhart

CHAPTER SIXTEEN

CONFRONTING ANXIETY AND TRAUMA: PART OF THE PROCESS

This next section is focused on leveraging ACT (Acceptance and Commitment Therapy) tools, based on the information that was outlined in Chapter 13. In no way am I pretending to be a psychologist! However, the nature of the relationship we have to money requires that we use some tools to understand the motivations and reasons behind our behaviors. This framework can be quite helpful. The principle, at the heart of this process, is that to create a rich and full life, we must accept that pain, loss, frustration, disappointment, and failure come along with it. To develop stronger psychological flexibility is to see that you have choices. You need to separate yourself from "I am" statements and instead choose "I am noticing that ..."

Secondly, does the behavior that you are choosing get you closer or farther away from what you want? We all have hard-wired messages, values, memories, and sensations that will block our clarity at times. But rather than avoiding something because it has created past trauma or bad feelings, is there something we can do differently, or choose differently, to get us closer to what we want? Exploring our choices more fully is really important. This is often the stage that most people shortchange. It is good to really explore all options and choices, even if it is to dismiss them as something we do not want to do. When we take time to be more mindful of our choices, we tend to create more positive behaviors for ourselves and a better result for ourselves and others that may be impacted by our choices and behaviors. By really exploring whether the choices get us closer or farther away from what we want, we should feel and act in ways that are more aligned with our desired outcome.

| | |

In order to get through the stages, it is helpful to see the circular chart of decision making presented here and try to control more of our responses to be thoughtful and intentional.

The Circular Nature of Our Behaviors

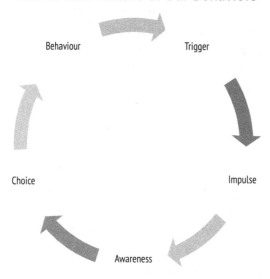

Behaviour   Trigger

Choice   Impulse

Awareness

Triggers lead to Impulses, which leads to an Awareness (of our personal connection and emotion), which leads to (understanding that we have) Choices, which then leads to (in its best form) a Behavior response that is intentional and clear.

Many people get hung up on having an impulsive behavioral response before they have taken the time to build an awareness and appreciation for identifying several potential responses before choosing one. When we take the time to analyze and consider different points of view or courses of action, we build more constructive behaviors for both the short term and the long term.

I I I

When our son was young and playing ice hockey, we regularly saw parents misbehaving and treating referees with disrespect. Reflecting on what they experienced, the kids would then blame the referees if they lost the game. As we used to say to our son, if the team had played better, scored more, and allowed fewer goals against them, there would be no blaming the referees. Perhaps it is more constructive to think about what you could do better to help your team win rather than placing blame elsewhere!

As a woman who was raised traditionally, and just assumed that I would be compensated fairly for my work, I understand that many women are poor negotiators on their own behalf. They are fierce when it comes to advocating for associates, friends, and family, but when left on their own, they turn into mush. We must visit this and reframe our relationship with negotiating on our behalf.

| | |

I once had a psychologist who had me put a nicked-up hockey puck on my desk to remind me that I am tough and need to negotiate like I play hockey. This meant being prepared, persistent, scrappy, focused, and intense.

In the work world, we need to think in a framework of goals and resilience. When we train to make the most of our skills and help our team, we need to think about how we contribute individually, and as part of the team, in order to fuel the success of the firm. This is true for both performance and culture. We cannot ignore one at the expense of others. As we prepare to negotiate, we assess our hard skills and contributions but also our soft skills, values, and contributions to culture. We may need to ask others for help in this assessment. Then we need to look at the competitive landscape. What is competitive compensation, benefits, and alignment toward individual goals and firm goals? We need to do our preparation and training before we jump into a negotiation.

| | |

The challenge may be that we have been treated unfairly in the past. That often brings on defensiveness or feelings of inadequacy. Sometimes if we have experienced trauma around a money choice or situation in the past, we continue to carry that with us. Anytime something similar happens, we feel inadequate again, like we felt during that previous trauma. However, we need to reframe the dialogue, as outlined above, to take the emotion out and to get ourselves to a better place where we are in a position of strength. Never is a negotiation just about the money! We must articulate our personal value as a teammate and individual. We must OWN OUR BEHAVIOR!

Financial Abuse

"No matter how difficult and painful it may be, nothing sounds as good to the soul as the truth."

—Martha Beck

Over the years, I have seen, much too often, forms of financial abuse between partners and spouses, or between generations. This can take many forms, including verbal abuse or taking control of a person's money and preventing him or her from accessing it. Financial abuse is a pattern of behaviors that is meant to control or intimidate a partner and can occur even if the abused person were the one to earn the money. Typical actions include ruining your credit score, refusing to pay household bills, guilting you into paying his or her loans, and undermining the household budget. It may also include sabotaging or behaving in ways that make you feel or become financially unstable or dependent. It is also important to know that financial abuse often occurs alongside other forms of domestic violence. In a small 2018 study from the Institute of Women's Policy Research (IWPR), 164 people living in shelters were surveyed across 11 states and Washington, DC. Of those people, 70% of the survivors had dealt with at least five types of abuse, including financial, physical, sexual, emotional, and stalking. Financial abuse often means an inability to leave because almost every option of independence, including transportation, food, shelter, etc., requires monetary resources.

For certain, financial abuse is as detrimental and trauma-producing as any other form of abuse. It is as silent and isolating as any form of abuse, as well. If you do not break the abusive cycle, you will continue to fall prey to the abuser who holds this power over you.

I I I

Many years ago, I went to a couple's home for a meeting. I had always known the husband to be a strong personality, demanding and forceful. But I had no idea how harmful he could be until I was in his home with his wife. He constantly sent conflicting messages and put her down.

The conversation was very circular. He would say something that sounded supportive like "Honey, this is your money, and I want you to feel like you can make your own decisions." Then, not minutes later, she would ask a question, and he would say, "That is a stupid question. You should know better." At this point, she would get teary and walk into the other room. Then he would start the cycle again by saying she should come back and work with me since it was her money. Staying in the room, he would then make another cruel remark when she reengaged. It was a horrifying experience for all of us, but obviously, most of all, for her. I struggled to find a way to free her from the abusive behavior.

| | |

A few years later, we had made some progress building her confidence and her resiliency to his behavior so that she was making some decisions around her funds. Then the strangest thing happened. I was notified by the custodian of the assets that she had passed away. Sadly, the first place my mind went was, *Did he move from verbal abuse to physical abuse?* Pushing that aside, I called the house to express my condolences. Imagine my surprise when she answered the phone. It turns out that he had wanted control of her funds, so he told the custodian that she had died. What the husband didn't realize was that saying his wife had died automatically triggers the custodian to put a freeze on the accounts until they receive a copy of the death certificate and postmortem instructions, per her estate. So, he still could not get control! But how horrific is this chapter of the story?

While the story that I just told is clearly awful, financial abuse can be much more subtle. Sometimes it is a spouse saying, I am having trouble in my business, incurred extensive debt, and need to use your personal savings or retirement money to pay my bills. Often, this happens later in life, when earning potential is reduced due to fewer years left to work. This is *not* acceptable.

| | |

Clearly, a couple needs to be on the same page and talking about their finances before such a crisis happens. While more subtle, this second example is also financial abuse because it is taking power from one partner and giving it all to the other partner. But that partner/spouse giving their money to the other to pay the debt now risks being able to support themselves later in life. For women, this is especially true because we live longer and, on average, out-live a male spouse by 15 years. This is a risk too high to take. Instead, like any other form of relationship, there needs to be mutual satisfaction, good communication, and shared values and accountability.

Trusted Partners

Over the years, I have done a better job as a coach for others than as an advocate for myself in negotiating for a job or position and for monetary reward. Maybe it is much easier for me to negotiate for others because I can focus on the facts and details without being clouded by emotion. Many women fall short in negotiations because we feel that we should get what we are worth. Sadly, it most often doesn't work that way. But our progress toward closing the pay gap and achieving pay parity depends on us learning better strategies for negotiating.

In order to help take the emotion out of the negotiation, it is best to follow a data-oriented approach, including job responsibilities, success metrics, milestones, and corresponding rewards for reaching those milestones. It is also critical to look at benefits that may be less obvious but critically important, like health care, disability insurance coverage, supplemental life insurance, the depth of retirement benefits and offerings, perks, and resources. In addition, reporting position, compensation expectations in terms of raises, bonuses, and other incentive plans, and career track clarity should be outlined up-front before accepting the position or promotion.

I I I

If you are contemplating a change or have multiple offers, a good strategy is to develop a framework to assess comparative jobs with salary and employment benefits. Most people focus so much on the salary that they do not fully take advantage of negotiations or explore benefits that can be worth more than money and improve quality of life.

When you have a financial wellness advisor help in the negotiating process, they will typically look at everything that encompasses the job and employment. They will also look at how its benefits relate to you, and, if you have a family, how they may benefit. After that, you can compare your salary and benefits to industry standards and other comparative information. This helps take some emotion out of the decision and focus more on the important choices and decisions with good data and information.

I I I

When a young woman I know was negotiating her first job, she was focused on salary. Realizing that she was at the top of the range that the CEO was willing to pay, I asked about other areas of value to her that might be negotiable. She quickly dismissed some of my ideas, fearing she would offend the CEO by asking probing questions. As a CEO myself, I explained the situation from that vantage point. I was recommending that she ask for membership dues to be paid for her for two industry organizations where she could be visible to help promote the services of her company. I told her that for her professional development, these organizations would be quite helpful. I pointed out that if I were in her CEO's shoes, I would view this as showing initiative and an interest in helping the company. I prepared her for the conversation, and despite her fears, she reported back that not only was her CEO willing to pay the membership dues, but also pay her overtime, parking, and any other related costs for events. The financial benefit was worth thousands of dollars to her. Although this was not part of her salary, it was clearly a good benefit for her.

A few years ago, a client was exploring three different opportunities. I used a comparative framework to look at salary, benefits, and other key decisions or opportunities. Her preferred job was to go with a company where the CEO might retire in three to five years, which could put her position at risk due to the change in leadership. The salary negotiation had hit a limit, so I suggested she ask to remain in some high-profile national organizations as a speaker and thought leader. In negotiations, this is not part of the salary, and as such, it was viewed differently. While it was still a substantial expense, it was classified in a different area of expenses, so it would not be a challenge to their compensation structure. Importantly, her CEO appreciated that this kept their company in a high, positive profile, and it would help both her and the company. She happily agreed to this expense. When the CEO retired a few years later, our client was scooped up immediately by another firm because she was visible nationally and viewed as a leader in the industry.

| | |

Negotiation is about preparation and purpose. It is about understanding how the other party can mutually benefit, if you are successful. It is not all about you but rather how you can contribute to the greater good through your own success. Yes, it is also about understanding what you need to have in place to be successful and conveying that message in an even, thoughtful, and informative way. Additionally, knowing what their limits are and how to position things in a beneficial light for all is a part of the process. At the end of the day, it is about setting you both up for success.

"Doubt is a killer. You just have to know who you are and what you stand for."

—Jennifer Lopez

CHAPTER SEVENTEEN

FAMILY AWARENESS CHALLENGES, BARRIERS, AND OPPORTUNITIES

Generational Challenges

Today elder fraud and cyber fraud are rampant. Sadly, these fraudsters prey on our elders, who may have declining cognitive and reasoning functions. At the other end of the spectrum are young people who have never received any financial education and are racking up debt that will take years or potentially decades to pay off. If you have followed along in this book, then you are developing your own healthy relationship with money. You need to broaden this dialogue within the generations of your family. As we have discussed, getting "financially naked" is scary, but avoiding it can be disastrous.

Help your family to see that there are advisors who can help coach you through the process.

Here are some excellent ways to start.

Your Children

You can teach your children about your values and choices without having to go into a great deal of financial detail. Perhaps an example would be helpful to illustrate how this conversation might be framed.

| | |

As I explained in Chapter 13, in 2007-2008 during the market and economic downturn, our children were relatively young—10, 13, and 15 years old. They heard at school about mothers and fathers losing their jobs. They knew that my career was in the financial services industry and that things sounded bad in conversations with their friends. Like most people, we had allowed expenses to build without budgeting because the economy was good. We needed to pull in the reins but also help our kids understand the framework of our financial decisions by relating it to our values.

Our children were in private school, which has always been a priority in our family. We have sacrificed other luxuries to provide this experience for our children. That was the first thing we talked to them about regarding how our lifestyle would change. We told them that we planned to cut a lot from other areas of our lives to keep them in their current schools. That was our priority.

| | |

Our second priority was family time. We would still go on vacation, but we would drive instead of flying, which would save not only the cost of airfare but also rental car fees. We told them the cost would be about 60% lower for us to drive instead of fly and gave them a ballpark of what that number would be so that they could understand the math better. We would still do things together on the weekends that involved travel, attending some of the great venues and offerings of our city, because time together was a gift for us all. Family dinners were still a priority, but we would limit going out and plan more dinners at home. We explained the difference in the cost of meals, as well.

Then we talked about the things that would be cut because we did not value them as highly. These include cable TV, discretionary purchases like "American Girl Dolls" and accessories, and our family wants versus needs. These were not easy discussions, but truthfully, the kids were relieved. When there is stress, everyone jumps to conclusions that are often off target. They knew the plan, and we were all aligned in our priorities.

As time goes on, you should continue to have "family meetings." These should always focus on values and goals as your compass. Once there is a good dialogue around those topics and the meaning of family "wealth," then you can talk more about particulars of plans for financial resources. This should also include healthcare expectations and planning. Legal responsibilities such as who will be assigned the power of attorney or serve as a trustee or executor should also be discussed when they are of appropriate ages.

| | |

As time goes on, it is important to introduce adult-age children to the key family advisors. Your children and all family members need to build their own relationships with these individuals. Similarly, the advisors need to invest in really getting to know and understand everyone in the family. This should happen both inside the meetings through inclusive questioning and participation and outside of the family meetings through downtime or breaks when a more casual conversation occurs. It is critical that the advisors on the team create an interactive dialogue that assures everyone is heard.

It is also important to prepare adult children for some of the decisions that they will need to make upon reaching "age" in their state. In some states the age is 21, but most states are at 18 years of age. For example, at age 18, parents no longer have healthcare and financial power of attorney. Rather, the young adult now needs to "assign" those rights through their own healthcare power of attorney and power of attorney. Similarly, if they have retirement accounts, including an Individual Retirement Account, it is important to know who they would like as their beneficiaries. While many kids still feel that their parents should be in those roles, a good advisor will help walk you through a variety of options because there can be tax consequences or other unforeseen conflicts. So, beginning these conversations between the advisors and family members both independently and in the context of the greater family conversation or meeting is a good role for the outside advisor. It helps ensure that everyone has a voice but that the plans are integrated and conflict-free.

I I I

Family meetings are about both the family relationships and goals, but also about the business of the family. Setting aside this time is important. Many families also develop a family mission statement to flesh out their shared values and priorities. This tool can convey more and more about how you use your money and why. Often the younger generation is relieved to have a clearer picture and better understanding of the future. For the parents, you can leverage these moments to have some of the harder conversations about your future and what you have planned for, so that your children or beneficiaries will not worry. You can also use it as an opportunity for the younger generation to take on responsibilities. By using this type of format and structure, you are developing good role modeling for them to use with their future partners or families as well.

Your Parents

To say that talking about money is emotional is an understatement. As parents age, we must begin to have nonthreatening discussions about their plans. Often a good way to start is by showing your own financial vulnerability and talking through your plans. Second, recognize what they have provided for you and how it has helped you to get where you are today. This positive talk helps release cortisol, which is the hormone that opens our minds and makes us more receptive.

Truthfully, the best time to start this conversation is when your parents are in their mid to late 50s. If this age range has already passed, be assured that having these conversations earlier is better than later. When we are in our 50s, we have more life experience and more experience with financial decision making. We understand that whether it is retirement, loss of a loved one, or challenges in healthcare, we must have a plan. As we experience the cognitive decline of friends and family, we become acutely aware of our own vulnerability.

| | |

Financial decision making is one of the first skills to deteriorate as we age, and as such, our cognitive abilities decline, as well. Discussions regarding cognitive decline are often fraught with anxiety for all involved. It can lead to defensiveness and despair. Lack of a plan can lead to a conflict among adult children in the family, which causes further stress and concern. A State Street Global Advisor study reports that while 72% of advisors indicate that they provide investors with information and support about the potential impact of aging on financial decisions, only 27% of investors are satisfied with the information and support given to them by advisors about the potential effect of aging on financial decisions. Further, only about 39% of investors believe that they have a suitable plan for when their decision making becomes diminished.

The need is clear. But the challenge is that at this stage, there is a full return to the Fear Zone because we are in a new chapter of life. There are many psychological hurdles in dealing with cognitive decline. In 2016, State Street Global produced a report on the Impact of Aging on financial decisions that was insightful. The biggest fears of their aging clients included loss of their independence. Clients are concerned about the possibilities of denial of their own mortality, lack of self-awareness of their cognitive decline, and corresponding poor financial decision making. This leads elders to be very vulnerable and in danger of taking important actions that cannot be undone.

| | |

Having these discussions is difficult. It is critical to have these planning discussions before some of these judgment issues arise with elders. Family meetings to address a plan for a loved one's decline are critical, and the need to do it before you are in crisis is imperative.

In addition to having these discussions as a family, it is critical to engage with your advisors so that they can understand the impact of all decisions on relationships and family finances. In the same report from State Street Global, their findings indicated that advisors were also not having difficult conversations with clients and their family members. In fact, while 46% of elders had discussed planning for death with family, only 25% had discussed it with their financial professional. Similar gaps were also reported for planning for retirement, inheritance, long-term care, cognitive decline, and other likely life events. How can that be?

| | |

As indicated, the data shows that advisors are also thinking they are doing a better job than clients believe they are! So, facilitating family meetings and having consistent building conversations around these issues is critical. This is the hardest work we probably ever do as advisors. But we need to help families find a way to have a conversation around safety, long-term vitality, and relevancy. This is where a financial wellness architect can really help a family address these tough issues.

Whether these conversations involve a financial professional and/or therapist/psychologist, every family needs help with this challenging transition.

My father was brilliant and fabulous with finances ... until he was not. He was diagnosed with Alzheimer's, and I quickly learned that while I thought I knew a fair amount about this horrid disease and elder cognitive decline strategies, I was naïve and relatively clueless. First, watching a loved one lose their brilliant mind and all that goes with it, like the ability to read and have rich conversations, is heartbreaking. Over time they lose everything they know and love. My father eventually lost his ability to speak and even to chew and swallow. This is a cruel disease.

Most families are in crisis without a plan. They are dealing with their own emotions while trying to make changes with someone who cannot make thoughtful decisions. Some elders can become belligerent and financially dangerous. The elderly, on top of all their diminishing abilities, are vulnerable to scams and other frauds. They can lose everything because there are many con artists out there preying on them every day.

| | |

Fortunately, my father was a planner. He ran some private investment funds and put a plan in place for his succession so that all his investors would be protected. He had a succession plan for all the boards that he served on and played a key role in their financial success. My father chose solid, trustworthy people to step in to help the businesses and his family. He put together everything needed to support and take care of my mother—except for his presence, which was her biggest loss but not something he could control.

Despite having this all in place, my father became belligerent at times, and his judgment became quite poor: the disease was taking its toll. However, since he had the plans in place, and the authorities set up, we could help make decisions to keep him and the family safe and protected.

What no one ever educated my mom and me on was how hard it would be to make decisions as a caregiver. Even practical decisions are fraught with emotion and anxiety. We may have known what needed to be done, but it did not make it easier as we gradually saw his world becoming more and more limited. Taking away his car keys, because he was a liability on the road, was probably one of the worst days of my life.

| | |

My father and I had always been very close and respectful of each other's opinions and recommendations. However, with Alzheimer's, one of the first things to go is judgment. My father, who had been an excellent driver for years, though he still was good behind the wheel. But he was driving over curbs, hitting things, and generally a terror on the road. He was a danger to himself and others. Yet, he still thought he was a good driver. When we had a doctor tell him he had to stop driving, he just decided never to return to that physician, and he kept driving. Eventually, we had to take the keys, tell him he was going to hurt someone—for example, one of us and himself—and the risk was just too high. We had to hide the keys because he was smart and resourceful. It was awful. He would not talk to me for days. I was the bad guy who had taken away his keys and his independence.

While many things had been planned, the issue of taking away Dad's independence to drive himself wherever he wanted to go was something we did not plan well for, sadly. We all avoided dealing with it because we knew my father would not react well. As always, avoidance led to escalation and a less than optimal outcome.

| | |

A critical element at this stage is to try and get everyone on the same page. Do not go down this path alone. There are excellent resources. Ask for help and guidance and find others who have gone through a similar experience. You will need the support!

I will forever be thankful that we had most of the important conversations around plans and succession when he was still vibrant and engaged. It was helpful to know what he wanted and know that we were making choices based on his desires. Now, making decisions with and for my mom, his widow, I have better support systems in place. She and I often discuss what her options are, or will be, and what the potential consequences might be for each decision. Not everyone will agree with the choices, but talking them through while she still has her full faculties is critical. Making plans when your parents still have cognitive ability is imperative. Later, their judgment is not as clear, and emotions escalate for everyone involved. Having a plan outlined and understood by several family members, outlining what the elder's intentions and desires are, is vitally important.

"Everything you want to be, you already are.
You're simply on the path to discovering it."

—Alicia Keys

CHAPTER EIGHTEEN

FINANCIAL WELLNESS AT DIFFERENT AGES AND STAGES: AN ASSESSMENT TOOL

The following assessment is just that; a test at one point in time. This can be an objective starting place but clearly must be taken in conjunction with all the other steps in the Lumination Process. This assessment is meant to find gaps and opportunities to help create dialogues and plans. Financial wellness is a dynamic state of financial health and its intersection with your life goals. In no way does a high score on this assessment indicates complete financial security. It is one tool and part of a process to identify the next steps and priorities.

Financial wellness looks different at different ages. What could be favorable at one age may not still be relevant or adequate at another stage. Quite simply, life interferes and causes setbacks that might require delaying the next stage or its requirements. It's important to have a plan to help "catch up" with your plans at different stages of life.

| | |

The stages are developed in sequence and represent "typical" progression. In the first assessment for Early Career, an individual is building their foundation for the future. The concept is to get the elementary building blocks in place to leverage for future needs and stages.

Stage 2 is Mid-Career, when more of a person's life ambitions are coming into play. At this stage, we need more balance of real-life demands and requirements. Typically, in this stage, we have more to juggle and more choices to make on how resources are allocated. We are in a higher consuming state of life and, as such, our financial resources are committed to different areas of life. This stage for most will include their 30s and 40s. What is important at any stage, and especially in Mid-Career, is to keep looking toward the assessment goals of the next step. It is never too early to start thinking about the next stage.

The Late Career stage can be most affected by when you had children and if you have the demands of senior care, as well. But a key need at this stage is to ensure that assets are being accumulated and reviewed for growth, balanced with capital preservation, to support you in your life post-career. This is the stage where life can deal us the most unexpected challenges. An important part of the assessment at this point is to be clear about your priorities and, if sacrifices are being made, what the plan is to get back on track.

| | |

Pre-Retirement can also be a time when people choose to have a lower income job to pursue a more fulfilling passion. "Encore" careers are often a good decision but it is necessary to take into account any changes in income assumptions, to prepare for the years when the person is no longer working. Historically, I have seen joy, and honestly, a healthier lifestyle, come from a change to a more flexible or more rewarding job or career. So, from a financial wellness standpoint, a career change is a good decision if the assessment and planning indicate the individual or family can support their goals and needs in later stages.

The Legacy Building and Generation Sharing Stage is often the most overlooked period. Many individuals and families think about the use of resources at this stage. However, they often do not focus on the family legacy, preserving the history and ensuring that values and wishes are shared and understood. If time and facilitated dialogue do not occur, extreme and undesired measures may be taken in health decisions, depleting financial resources and the quality of life's last chapter. Family stories and history can be lost forever. Conversely, families can enrich the lives of generations by sharing stories, important valuables, and values.

Again, these assessments are meant to drive dialogue, planning, and more comprehensive knowledge about risk management. While the stages build on one another, at any time, you can be working on the next stage or having to remediate for something that caused a backsliding. That is life.

FINANCIAL WELLNESS ASSESSMENT

Early Career (Ages 20–29)

Foundation Building

- ☐ I review my bills and statements for accuracy regularly.
- ☐ I have consistent income which covers my basic expenses.
- ☐ I have health insurance.
- ☐ I have at least $1,000 in a savings account for emergencies.
- ☐ I add to my emergency savings account every month with the goal of eventually getting to 6 months' worth of must-pay expenses.
- ☐ I have a spending plan/budget, and I monitor my expenses.
- ☐ I use an electronic or digital system to manage/stay on top of my expenses.
- ☐ I know my short-term and long-term financial goals.
- ☐ I know my credit score and what affects it, and I work to establish, maintain, or improve it.
- ☐ I do not carry any high-interest debt.
- ☐ I pay my credit cards off every month.
- ☐ I am contributing enough to my retirement plan at work—401(k) or 403(b), etc.—to get the full employer match.
- ☐ I am using a Roth 401(k) or contributing to a Roth IRA.
- ☐ If I have student loans, I have a plan to pay them off.
- ☐ If I'm a renter, I have renter's insurance.
- ☐ I have a will, a power of attorney, and Healthcare Power of Attorney in place and communicated to those involved.
- ☐ I know my investing personality (hands-on vs. hands-off) and have a simple investing strategy.

☐ If I'm married or living with my partner, we have full financial disclosure and have open discussions on how we manage money together.

☐ By my late 20s/early 30s, I am able to buy a first home, if that's my goal.

☐ I have disability income insurance through work or independently.

☐ I know the impact of fees on my investments and minimize fees when possible.

☐ I have personal liability insurance.

☐ I have a healthy relationship with money.

☐ If I would like to work with a financial advisor, I know how to find an advisor who is a fiduciary and works on a fee-only basis and how to check their background and credentials.

Mid-Career: (30–44)

Real Life Requires More Balance and Adjustments

☐ I answered yes to all the items that apply to me in my early career (20s).

☐ I have a will (with guardianship provisions for my kid(s), if I have them),

☐ I own my home (if that is a goal) and have a competitive rate on my mortgage.

☐ If anyone depends on my income for their lifestyle (spouse, kids), I have adequate life insurance.

☐ I have a trusted advisor(s) to assist me with financial decisions.

☐ I am saving at least 15% in my 401(k), including my employer match. If I'm not there yet, I am using the automatic rate escalator feature in my plan to get there over time.

☐ I consistently spend less than I earn and avoid accumulating high-interest debt

☐ I have a systematic plan to save for shorter-term goals, such as vacations, home maintenance, and taxes

☐ My transportation expenses (car, insurance, gas, and parking) are less than 8% of my income

☐ My housing expenses (mortgage/rent, utilities, insurance, and maintenance) are less than a third of my income.

☐ I'm maximizing tax-advantaged accounts for healthcare (HSA or FSA) and childcare (FSA) if needed.

☐ If I have kids, I know how much college may cost, and I am funding education accounts even if it is only in small amounts. However, I'm not funding education accounts at the expense of funding my own retirement.

☐ I evaluate my insurance coverage every year.

☐ I keep track of all my charitable gifts and other tax records.

☐ I pay my taxes on time and have the withholding set appropriately.

☐ I have run a retirement projection, and I know if I am on track or not for retirement at my desired age.

☐ I prepare for job interviews and promotions to ensure I am valued and understand how to improve, grow, and get paid what I am worth.

☐ My investments are well-diversified, and I have a consistent strategy.

☐ I have repaid my student loans if I had them.

☐ I maximize my employer benefit plans (all "free" ones) and review additional offerings with my advisor.

Late Career (50s)

Accumulation and Growth

☐ I answered yes to all the items that apply to me in my early career (20s) and mid-career (ages 30–44).

☐ According to my retirement projection, I am on track for my retirement goal.

☐ I am maximizing my retirement plan contributions.

☐ I am maximizing my benefit plans and tax savings strategies consistent with my priorities and values.

☐ If I have children in high school, I understand the college financial aid process and what affects the financial aid formula.

☐ I have a complete estate plan (will, health care directive, health care and financial powers of attorney).

☐ I have a charitable giving strategy for short and long term.

☐ I know my investment risk tolerance and invest accordingly by seeking advice from my advisors.

☐ My advisor or I monitor my investments and rebalance at least annually.

☐ I am building savings outside of my retirement accounts, and I am investing there using tax-efficient strategies.

☐ I or my advisor has reevaluated the pre-tax vs. Roth question given my current income and time until retirement.

☐ I know how I'll fund long-term care needs in retirement.

☐ I have increased my emergency savings overtime to cover larger needs, such as a longer period of unemployment or reduced income.

☐ My assets are adequately protected (trusts, umbrella liability policy, LLC for rental property, etc.).

☐ I have discussed my parents' financial situation and wishes for health care with them.

☐ I know in general where I want to live in retirement.

☐ I spend time reflecting on how to enjoy my assets in an affordable way.

Preparing for Simplification and Financial Independence: (Ages 55+)

☐ I answered yes to all the items that apply to me in my early career (20s), mid-career (ages 30–44), and late-career (ages 45–54) stages.

- ☐ If I have multiple advisors, and they are proactive and collaborative, holding my best interests in mind.
- ☐ I have a well-documented estate plan, and I understand how it aligns with my wishes.
- ☐ I have a plan to reallocate my investments between now and retirement to meet my goals and needs appropriately.
- ☐ I have a plan for my retirement accounts at retirement and an investment strategy for meeting my spending needs.
- ☐ I know when I want to retire, or if I'll retire in stages, and what I plan to do in retirement.
- ☐ I have a backup plan in case I leave the workforce earlier than expected due to illness or layoff.
- ☐ I have a plan to pay long-term care expenses.
- ☐ If I plan to retire before 65, I know what I'll do for health insurance prior to Medicare kicking in.
- ☐ I understand the decisions I'll have to make for Social Security and Medicare.
- ☐ If I am eligible for a pension, I know the pros and cons of my distribution choices.
- ☐ If I'm not planning to stay in my current home, I have a plan to move and/or downsize.
- ☐ I have clearly communicated my wishes with family, both verbally and in writing.

Legacy and Generational Sharing

- ☐ My family meets annually to discuss our history, values, and priorities.
- ☐ I have communicated to my family any items that are earmarked for a beneficiary and the important stories that they should know about that item.
- ☐ My legal documents are reviewed regularly, and especially if any family changes (loss) occurs.

☐ I understand the different responsibilities of my executor and trustee(s) and feel confident that I have communicated my intent, their roles, and they have agreed to serve.

☐ I have communicated and documented my wishes for caregiving when I am no longer able to care for myself.

☐ I have communicated to one or more family members or friends where all important documents, passwords, and/or safety deposit box keys are located.

☐ I have distributed to my family a list of my key advisors and their contact information. They know who should be the "first" call.

☐ I have signed and executed documents with my financial institutions and custodians indicating who can access my funds on my behalf should I become incapacitated.

☐ I have given the individual who has my HPOA and Living Will a copy of any long-term care policies or additional healthcare information that may be permanent.

☐ I know not to give any personal information, including my Social Security number or financial information to anyone over the phone.

*"It took me quite a long time to develop a voice,
and now that I have it, I am not going to be silent."*

—Madeleine Albright

CHAPTER NINETEEN

FINDING YOUR FINANCIAL WELLNESS ARCHITECT

A financial wellness architect is a coach or advisor who spends the time to understand your values, looks at all aspects of your life with you as outlined, and then helps you build a plan to use your financial capital and human capital to reach your dreams and aspirations. I use the term *architect* because the term *financial wellness advisor* may be too common and indicates a more passive role. The architect is taking a more proactive and constructive role. They are focused beyond advice and to a deeper meaning, foundational work and coaching. I liken it to having an instructor in a class versus a coach who spends more time with you and who knows you better. A financial wellness architect has technical skills but also emotional intelligence and therapeutic and motivational coaching skills. A financial wellness architect believes that every individual and family is different and needs to develop their own plan and journey. They believe in the Lumination approach to developing your Wealth Life Plan.

Sadly, the financial services industry is the most despised industry by women, beating out used car salespeople! A 2018 Edelman Trust Barometer Research study indicated that only 54% of consumers trust financial services companies and that we are the least trusted industry. The reasons are obvious, as most financial advisors just want to talk about the money, an "asset grabbing" approach. These financial advisors often start by asking how much money you have before even understanding what is important to you.

| | |

For women, the statistics are even worse. In a 2018 study by Pimco, over half of the women said that the financial services industry does not reflect their lifestyles or services. Evaluation of performance is tied to meeting a woman's own standard versus beating an investment benchmark. Most important, financial stability and planning, for both long-term and short-term goals, and achieving financial independence all take precedence over retirement planning. This book is meant to show you that you can find those advisors who want to focus on your financial wellness versus just investments. Here is how you do it!

It is time to demand and expect more from financial advisors. First, the relationship should be a mutually satisfying relationship, much like sex! It is not about your consent or "giving in," but rather about your working together and your feeling appreciated and understood. If you are in a relationship with an advisor now that is not fun and feels unhealthy, then take a "time out." You can research to find a coach who will be focused on you and your wellness. In the industry, there is a term called the Fiduciary Standard. The Fiduciary Standard dictates that this type of advisor must act with care, due diligence, and knowledge in the best interest of the client. As a result, the first hurdle is to find an advisor who is bound by the Fiduciary Standard.

I I I

Many advisors today are mostly focused on investment management or money management. They may be getting rewarded for selling a "product," including certain mutual funds, insurance policies, or they may receive commissions for certain products.

You need to make sure that you are working with a fiduciary who is conflict-free. You have every reason to ask if they are a fiduciary, if they have any conflicts of interest, and how they are compensated. These are three very important questions. As you can see from the above wheel, they should be discussing all strategies in each part of the circle. A "fiduciary" is required to have a full understanding of you and your situation before making any decisions.

I I I

The next step is to use the questions in the Financial Wellness Assessment to find a coach who acts as a personal financial wellness architect. They will do an assessment, like we introduced earlier in the book, and convey their understanding of your values, goals, and aspirations, as well as your concerns and worries. When they interact with you, expect communication that includes stories and examples of work they have done to help others in a situation like yours. The focus should not be on the market and abstract aspects at this stage but on you, your pathways, and your choices. (Market and investment discussions should come much later in the process.) Your coach should also be able to explain any financial terms or issues in clear and simple language without a lot of jargon. Importantly, your advisor should make everyone in the family feel welcome in important discussions, no matter how much of the wealth they currently control. This should be an inclusive and thoughtful process to engage all.

Your Lumination plan should be revisited annually in a more abbreviated way. As we have shown, the plan should be built from the specific process where advisors work with you through a comprehensive dialogue. At the inception of your relationship and for each succeeding year, you can revisit your money values and money journey. You will also review your hopes, dreams, and aspirations for you and your family, any potential triggers or barriers, and what is causing you to worry. The next phase is to identify your two to three top priorities as you review the wheel of life. What is most important to you to accomplish in this next year? If you have a partner or spouse, it is important that you agree on these priorities! Only after this rich dialogue and conversation about your life and current needs have been fulfilled does the advisor turn to the technical side of your plan to raise other issues that may need to be addressed. Often, they coordinate these activities with your other advisors to create the most seamless process possible for you. Here, the financial wellness architect is also taking into account the current and next stage of life for you and your family. This phase may involve highlighting new issues and upcoming decisions, as illustrated in the Financial Wellness Assessment, and connecting you to those services or people.

Wealth Management Deliverables

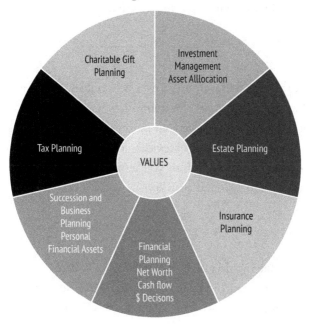

Your financial wellness architect integrates the above wealth management deliverables and areas with your life plan. They coordinate with your other advisors and bring in the technical expertise where needed to ensure all these pieces are coordinated in a way that supports your life plan. Every section in the wheel is interrelated with other areas of the wheel. It is critical that all are addressed and meet the person's evolving needs over different phases of life.

| | |

The third stage of this process is to have your next year's plan laid out on a calendar so that you know what to expect. For the busy executive, it might require getting the dates set up for meetings months in advance. For the widow, you may prefer to be a bit more flexible and not want to feel too scheduled. Either way, you and your coach are agreeing to the plan and approximate timing of meetings and deliverables to help you achieve your goals.

It is here that you will want to go over deliverables, meetings, topics, and other important issues. For example, where would you like more financial education for you or your family members? In addition, the Lumination Process is about providing connection and community for you and your family. Thus, you may need to be introduced to others who are in a similar situation.

| | |

Moreover, they should also be helping you to find advisors who will collaborate with you and lend their expertise to ensure that you have the best thinking and plans for you and your family. If your advisor is only discussing investment strategies, you have more work to do to find your financial wellness architect. If you have found an advisor that you feel looks at all aspects of your life, from the central priorities to a comprehensive plan involving all the circles above, you are on your way to financial wellness for you and your family. You want these professionals to clearly communicate with the other members of your advisory team, such as a CPA, estate planning attorney, insurance broker, banker, and others. The financial wellness architect is the one who has the deepest understanding of your whole life and is likely the coordinator of the team on your behalf.

At this point, we have identified a process to develop your "Lumination Plan" and how to find your own financial wellness architect or financial wellness advisor. You are on your way to living a well life.

"Only when we are brave enough to explore the darkness will we discover the infinite power of our light.

—Brené Brown

CONCLUSION

Leading a life that is consistent with one's values is the greatest predictor of happiness. If a family is to flourish today, and for multiple generations, they must explore their values, their own relationship to money, their hopes, dreams, and aspirations, their potential triggers and barriers, and share communication about what a well life means. The Lumination Process lays out a detailed but rewarding process of exploration and understanding. Your journey will be as rewarding as what this process can accomplish for you and your family.

When I started my journey as a financial wellness architect and advisor, I saw how poorly women were treated by our industry and by society. Yet they are often the member of the family who initiates the hardest and best conversations. They are often the ones that bring financial education and literacy to the next generation.

| | |

Statistically, we know that women control over 50% of the wealth in this country and are inheriting assets disproportionately to men. They have the power and the influence to drive social change.

Despite this growing influence and power, the financial industry has done little to improve its appeal to women. Financial advisors remain the most distrusted of any industry. It is time for dramatic change. It is time to create an experience that looks at the whole life plan: our history, our money journey, our hopes and dreams, our triggers and barriers, our stages of life, and how we can improve communication with those who are important to us in a meaningful way. The Lumination Plan, where you can develop your own journey and build your personal Wealth Life Plan, appeals to women and men who want a healthier and happier relationship with their human capital and financial capital to achieve their hopes and dreams.

| | |

Please pass this book on to others, especially those whom you admire and love, so that they, too, can flourish and enjoy more of what life has to offer. Thank you for reading this book and committing to a more meaningful future for you and your loved ones.

Please feel free to share your stories with us. We want to improve our process and your experience continually.

Dream Big
    + Take Action
        + Enjoy the Journey
            = Living an Abundant Life

APPENDIX

Key Questions for Finding a Financial Advisor

By Heather R. Ettinger

1. *Tell me a little bit about the firm's principals or partners and the length of your association with them.* This is always a good question to ask because you need to feel comfortable with the people that you are dealing with. Specifically, you want to know that they are committed to overseeing the successful stewardship of their clients' financial plan. You want to avoid firms where there is a high degree of turnover or lack of a clear and client-centered focus in their process. If they tend to recite facts and figures on product before they hear what your needs are, they are more interested in selling you than partnering with you. Find a team of professionals who can clearly articulate a mission and value proposition that resonates with you.

2. *Who is your target client?* You are looking for a firm that specializes in working with clients like you. This should be defined by niches or target groups such as widows, executives, divorcees, business owners, types of lifestyle need such as retirement planning, succession planning for business owners, charitable gift and legacy planning, and the complexity of the planning needs and perhaps target asset size. You want a firm that is thinking about both the financial and nonfinancial needs that are typical for what you will be facing over the next 10 to 20 years. For example, if the firm works with large institutional clients, their service experience would likely not provide you much value as an individual. You want to be a client that they seek and cherish!

3. *What is the psychographic of your target client?* I love this question because it gets to values and characteristics, often of both the advisor and team and the target client. If they can't articulate this, you might want to keep looking because they are just focused on getting clients. Those who have spent the time thinking this through are likely firms and advisors who want to develop a long-term relationship and partnership.

4. *Who will manage my financial affairs/money?* Most firms will have you meet a "face man," who is typically a person focused on selling the firm to prospective clients. However, you should ask to meet the person or, better yet, the team who will be working with you on a day-to-day basis and assist in managing your financial matters. Who will be answering your routine phone calls? Who will be providing you with information regarding your accounts?

   If they have a team structure, how are responsibilities designated on that team? Do you feel a sense of chemistry with those members? Gut instincts are not to be minimized!

5. *What are your "core" deliverables for every client?* If the firm is well run, they will have thought about making sure that clients

have some consistent experiences that help define their value proposition versus competitors in the marketplace. If you have established good relationships with outside advisors, you want to hear that they value the input of those advisors. As they describe their core deliverables, you want to hear references to a comprehensive process using resources and skill sets of different people as much as the actual deliverables, such as a financial plan, asset allocation, estate planning, etc. In other words, how they go about their planning process and how they integrate your financial and nonfinancial goals often determines the value of the actual deliverable.

6. *What is the scope of services that you offer?* You are looking for people who provide a broad scope of services from which you can work together and choose what is most appropriate for you. As noted above, they should have core deliverables that are consistent for every client. But they also should have the capability to go more in-depth or have relationships with outside resources to deal with more complicated and unique issues. For example, if you want to set up a family foundation or donor-advised fund, do they have relationships established with outside providers to implement that process? Do they have relationships with family business consultants or industrial psychologists to help with sticky emotional transitions with family businesses? These are some services that may be very important to the success of implementing your life plan.

7. *What is your investment philosophy? How do you make investment decisions?* What you are looking for is an approach that is consistent with your objectives, easily understood, and has a proven track record. You also want a firm that is not limited to their own investment product but will choose from many products to determine in an unbiased way what is best for you. Determine if they offer a diversified platform, which might include over 10 different asset classes or styles. "Open architecture" refers

to a firm having the freedom to select from any provider versus being limited to only their own products. The ability to choose from a wide platform may improve performance over time.

8. *Do you offer impact investing or ESG (Environmental, Social, Governance) portfolios?* If you are someone who wants your investments aligned with your values, this is the time to investigate if the firm has those offerings. You don't want them to do a "one-off" for you, but rather to have a defined process and platform for meeting this need.

9. *What is your strategy for protecting my money?* As you go through your selection process, you will find that most managers can look very good in a bull market—a rising stock market. However, the real test of a money manager is how they perform over the long haul, including performance in a bear market—a declining stock market. How does the manager protect the principal when stocks in general are losing value? After all, making money is only part of any investment advisor's job.

10. *Tell me about your firm's history relative to how the markets have changed over time.* As you look at a company's performance, you should also understand that it is important to engage managers who have a history of experience over many different years and during different stages of volatility in the economy. Living through various cycles in the market is important in determining what works through changing times rather than just the current time. Many people in the wealth and investment industry today like to talk about "winners and losers" over tactical and strategic changes that have been required by different circumstances and changes in both the domestic and worldwide economies. The late 1970s and the early 1980s were a much more challenging period for investment managers than even the tech decline in late 1999 through 2001. We also had the longer decline in 2008–2009 and now COVID-19 volatility. In looking at these periods of time, you will be able to determine which

firms produced a good track record during down markets as well as the up markets.

11. *How will the investment decisions in my portfolio differ from those of other clients of yours?* This question gets at the issue of how an investment manager tailors accounts to your specific needs and objectives, rather than buying or selling what they like or dislike without any differentiation as to what is appropriate for you. In other words, a client focused on generating income typically will have a differently structured portfolio than a client who is interested in long-term growth.

12. *How are your professionals compensated?* Obviously, if the professionals involved are compensated for new business without regard for client retention and satisfaction, they will be interested in "selling" you on the process rather than making sure you are a good fit long term for their firm. Be cautious of anything that has an upfront sales load or commission. Rather look for a relationship that is based on fees and value measured by performance relative to your needs and goals.

13. *How do you measure performance?* Most sales literature includes references to performance. Again, does the firm appear to be product driven, i.e., telling you all about how they manage investments and the returns, or are they focused on your goals and how they can provide a plan and services to help meet those goals? The best firms will talk about performance as measured by client satisfaction rates through client surveys, retention, and referrals from existing clients.

14. *What is your succession plan?* If a truck should hit you tonight, who will watch over my portfolio and address my needs? (Here, you are looking for depth and continuity within the organization.) You want to avoid the "superstar" firm because it puts you and your assets at greater risk. In addition, you typically want to work with a team so that you have familiarity with more than one person at the firm. Incidentally, firms that work in

teams tend to be much more efficient and service-oriented, as they can clearly designate responsibilities and accountability to make sure that your needs are met, and work is accomplished in a timely manner.

15. *How would you transition my current investments?* You want to make sure they are looking at your tax profile and estate plan. There is often the need to communicate with your other advisors and pay attention to detail. You do not want them to just sell the old and then buy what they like. You want to see a smooth transition plan with attention to taxes, fees, and estate and financial planning objectives.

16. *May I have references from clients who have been with your firm for several years who have objectives that are similar to mine?* This is a very wise question to ask since you want to make sure that the firm is dealing with clients who are similar to you and also that their clients have had successful relationships with the firm, resulting in a commitment to them over the years.

17. *Do you use your firm's services? Are you a client of your own firm?* If their services are as good as they say they are for individuals, then your potential advisor should be using them too, if applicable. Look for a clear and direct answer to this question.

18. *How do you communicate with clients?* You want to know how they will communicate and if it will include written performance reports and personal meetings. In addition, will they work with your other advisors such as tax advisors, estate planners, or charitable giving specialists, so that they really understand your unique personal profile and needs.

19. *What do you* not *do?* Many firms want to say they can be all things to all people. What will be more helpful is finding a firm that truly specializes in financial planning and then coordinates your other experts/advisors (estate planning attorneys, CPAs, insurance brokers, and investment managers) as they strategically create your master financial plan. You want an advisor or

firm that is clear about what they specialize in doing and what they will coordinate with outside experts and advisors. If they say they do it all themselves, you may get a "jack of all trade but master of none."

20. *Based upon our conversation, if we were to work together, what have you heard to be the most important aspects of our potential relationship?* Although these are suggested questions for you to ask, your meetings should be balanced with a healthy give and take. Your potential advisors should be asking you many questions to make sure that you are a good fit for their firm and that they understand the scope of services that you will need. You want to make sure they "listened" to you. If you are at a decision-making point and they cannot clearly articulate what your needs and priorities are, then you need to keep looking. Never forget, you must feel that you have found a trusted advisor who understands you and will coordinate the resources and experts required to fulfill your needs and objectives. No one cares about your money more than you do. You must feel a strong sense of trust with your financial partner.

ACKNOWLEDGEMENTS

Thank you to all the people who have helped to shine a light on my journey.

To my husband Jeff who has believed in me from the beginning and given me unwavering support as we made sacrifices and choices for me to pursue my dream.

To Pat, my inspirational fountain of creativity, challenge and clarity. You have been able to get at my core when I lost my way and get me back on track.

To my inspirational and visionary mentors, Marge, Janie, Ellie and Tracey. Your passion and purpose to educate and empower women has lived on in my heart and soul since we met many years ago.

To Ken and Kristen for seeing and sharing my vision and supporting me through many challenges and disappointments. For refocusing me on all that we have achieved and the lives that we have changed. For allowing me to be the crazy visionary, painting a new view of what the future could be.

To Suzanne, Kathleen McQ, KBK, and Roxanne for instantly connecting on our shared purpose of elevating women in all that we do.

To Tina for being my sounding board and steady guiding voice as we explore the why's of our world.

To my Fairport and Luma team and my posse for believing in me, especially when I had ideas ten years before our industry was ready for them!

To my dad who is still with me cheering me on and believing that I like him can make a greater impact on this world.

To my mom who is the most generous and thoughtful person I know.

To my three kids, Emily, Kelly and Henry, you have given me more joy than you will ever know. You have forgiven my mistakes and become people I truly admire.

To the women and men who have allowed me to dream BIG about how women can be the agents of social change, when we educate and empower them around their financial and human capital.

ABOUT HEATHER

As a champion for women and girls for over 30 years, Heather Ettinger is widely recognized for her unique experience and dedication to helping women build their financial acumen and wealth, culminating in the founding of Luma Wealth Advisors in 2017. She specializes in helping clients and their families create strategic financial plans to guide them through life transitions, such as the loss of a spouse, divorce and job changes and to align their resources around family values and impact in their communities.

Heather co-authored two studies about women and their unique needs entitled "Women of Wealth: Why Does the Financial Services Industry Still Not Hear Them?" and "Women of Wealth: What Do Breadwinner Women Want?" Heather has been featured in many publications including *The Wall Street Journal*, *Barron's* and *Bloomberg* and is a frequently requested speaker for industry associations, company women's initiatives and wellness events. For conceiving new ideas and tools that have propelled the financial industry forward, she was recognized as a 2019 "Icons and Innovators" honoree by *Investment News*. In 2019, she also proudly accepted The Ruth Bader Ginsburg award for advancing the aspirations of women from the Women's Vote Project.

Ms. Ettinger remains an ardent supporter of her alma maters including Dartmouth College, where she earned a B.A., and Laurel School for girls, where she now serves as an Emeritus Trustee. She is active with In Counsel with Women and the nationally recognized wealth management study group, Family Wealth Advisors Council. She has served on numerous non-profit and private company boards across a wide range of industries including distribution, manufacturing, technology, trust services, financial services and healthcare. Her most recent board service includes University Hospitals Health System, The Private Trust Company, Asurint One Source Technology, Schwab Institutional Services Advisory Board, and *Racing Towards Diversity.*

Ms. Ettinger considers raising her three children with her husband, Jeff, to be empathetic and giving adults to be her greatest and most rewarding accomplishment. Her favorite activities include playing ice hockey, skiing and hiking.

Interested in having a greater impact on your family giving or in your community, or learning more about aligning your financial resources for impact? Connect with Heather at heather@ heatherettinger.com or on social media.

heatherettinger.com
Facebook: financialwellnessarchitect
LinkedIn: @heatherettinger14
Twitter: @heatherinsight

VISIT HEATHERETTINGER.COM

Educational Resources + Thought Leadership +
Upcoming Speaking Engagements

For over 30 years Heather Ettinger has been connecting women and girls to resources to build their financial acumen and confidence. As an engaging, innovative and fun speaker, check out her upcoming speaking engagements, current highlights from well-known publications, and her features on podcasts, panels and webinars both in her industry and for women in general.

Heather has many tools in her toolbox including educational resources and a broad network of consultants and professionals to help you manage the life of you and your family. Serving generations of women and their families, she is a visionary leader and innovative thinker to all who connect with her.

An early pioneer of investing in women, Heather's core purpose is to educate and empower women so that they can be the agents of social change in their families, in their communities and/or in the greater world.

To participate in Heather's live sessions or book her to speak, please email heather@heatherettinger.com

Interested in having a greater impact on your family giving or in your community, or learning more about aligning your financial resources for impact? Connect with Heather on social media.

heatherettinger.com
Facebook: financialwellnessarchitect
LinkedIn: @heatherettinger14
Twitter: @heatherinsight

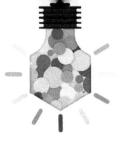

HIRE HEATHER

- *To be your keynote speaker*
- *Lead a training session on financial wellness*
- *Coach your female team members*

Award Winning • Inspiring • Entertaining • Impactful

Heather Ettinger has been hailed as dynamic and inspiring speaker. While she is nationally recognized for her expertise and experience on financial wellness for women, impactful philanthropy, navigating change as a leader and woman, what sets her apart is her approachable and warm style. Heather is not afraid to be vulnerable and share her successes and failures along the way. She is a great storyteller and wants to make every learning experience positive. You will leave her inspiring sessions with practical and easy to implement ideas and strategies.

To learn more about hiring Heather as your speaker, please visit heatherettinger.com.

ARE YOU READY TO BEGIN YOUR JOURNEY TO FINANCIAL WELLNES

Through real life scenarios, personal stories and practical applications, auth Heather Ettinger will take you on a journey to explore your past and present a help you design your intentional future. **LUMINATION** brings a refreshingly unic approach, tailored specifically for women, to examine their thoughts, emotions a life-long conditioning around money and life choices. This framework will shine a lig on your path to financial wellness and give you the tools and resources to gu you whenever life's planned and unplanned transitions change your course. \ can expect an inspiring and practical journey to your personal financial wellnes

Heather's goal is simple: To educate, empower and embrace women where th are today, and help take them to where they want to be in the future. Based over 35 years of coaching women and their families through financial transitic and life, Heather provides the essential guide for women to finally understand a unravel the money messages in their personal money journey; how to explore mor values and behavioral patterns around job/purpose, relationships, community, hea spirituality and play; and how to design and live their unique, intentional life that bring her (and her family) more joy.

"Heather Ettinger is the real deal and, in this book, she is a pure truth-teller. The prescript she writes for women surrounding our financial health is transparent and auther I saw my past, my present, and my opportunity to craft a smart financial future."

—**Margaret Mitchell,** President & CEO, YWCA Greater Clevela

HEATHER ETTINGER, a champion for women and girls for o 30 years, is widely recognized for her unique experience and d cation to helping women build their financial acumen and wea

As a published thought leader and frequently featured in su publications as the Wall Street Journal, Barron's, Bloomberg, a Your Teen Magazine, Heather is a highly requested speaker industry associations, company women's initiatives and welln events. For conceiving new ideas and tools that have propel the financial industry forward, she was recognized as a 2019 "Icons and Innovat honoree by Investment News. In 2019, she also proudly accepted The Ruth Bader Ginsbu award for advancing the aspirations of women from the Women's Vote Project.

Passionate about educating and empowering women and their families, Ms. Etting continually connects and collaborates with thoughtful partners and resour many of which can be found at **www.heatherettinger.com**.

ISBN 978-1-951591-43-

ACADEMY PRESS

9 781951 591434